YORK NOTES

AQA ENGLISH LANGUAGE AND LITERATURE

REVISION AND EXAM PRACTICE

STEVE EDDY

PEARSON

YORK PRESS

The right of Steve Eddy to be identified as the Author of this Work
has been asserted by him in accordance with the Copyright,
Designs and Patents Act 1988

YORK PRESS
322 Old Brompton Road, London SW5 9JH

PEARSON EDUCATION LIMITED
Edinburgh Gate, Harlow,
Essex CM20 2JE, United Kingdom
Associated companies, branches and representatives throughout the world

First published 2017

10 9 8 7 6 5 4 3 2

ISBN 978–1–2921–6978–1

Typeset by Carnegie Book Production
Printed in Slovakia

Text credits: 'Walking Away' from *The Gate and Other Poems* by Cecil Day Lewis reprinted by permission of Peters Fraser & Dunlop
(www.petersfraserdunlop.com) on behalf of the Estate of Cecil Day Lewis. Excerpt from "Follower" from OPENED GROUND:
SELECTED POEMS 1966-1996 by Seamus Heaney. Copyright © 1998 by Seamus Heaney. Reprinted by permission of Farrar, Straus and
Giroux, LLC and Faber and Faber Ltd. Excerpt from "Bayonet Charge" from COLLECTED POEMS by Ted Hughes. Copyright © 2003 by
The Estate of Ted Hughes. Reprinted by permission of Farrar, Straus and Giroux, LLC and Faber and Faber Ltd. 'Mother, any distance'
from *Book of Matches* by Simon Armitage reprinted by permission of Faber and Faber Ltd. Letter to *The Times*, 3 July 1905 – Bernard
Shaw reproduced by permission of The Society of Authors, on behalf of the Bernard Shaw Estate. Extract from *The Woman in
Black* by Susan Hill, published by Vintage Books © Susan Hill 1983. Reproduced by permission of Sheil Land Associates Ltd. 'Before
You Were Mine' from *Collected Poems* by Carol Ann Duffy. Published by Picador, 2015. Copyright © Carol Ann Duffy. Reproduced
by permission of the author c/o Rogers, Coleridge & White Ltd., 20 Powis Mews, London W11 1JN. 'War Photographer' from *New
Selected Poems* by Carol Ann Duffy. Published by Picador, 2009. Copyright © Carol Ann Duffy. Reproduced by permission of the
author c/o Rogers, Coleridge & White Ltd., 20 Powis Mews, London W11 1JN.

Photo credits: Nanisimova/Shutterstock for page 13 middle / Evgeny Karandaev/Shutterstock for page 16 bottom / Andresr/ ©
iStock for page 19 bottom / jjmillan/Shutterstock for page 20 middle / Genadi Dochev/Shutterstock for page 21 bottom / Steve
Oehlenschlager/Shutterstock for page 23 bottom / fotorince/Shutterstock for page 24 bottom / Kalcutta/Shutterstock for page 28
bottom / Fabien Monteil/Shutterstock for page 29 bottom / topseller/Shutterstock for page 31 bottom / irabel8/Shutterstock for page
32 bottom / Mike Joppe/ Shutterstock for page 37 top / jukurae/Shutterstock for page 39 bottom / conrado/Shutterstock for page 40
top / antoniodiaz/Shutterstock for page 41 bottom / jaymast/Shutterstock for page 42 bottom / mgfoto/© iStock for page 43 bottom
/ lbarrosphoto/© iStock for page 46 middle / Intrepix/Shutterstock for page 47 bottom / M. Ali Khan/Shutterstock for page 51 bottom
/ Inga Locmele/Shutterstock for page 56 bottom / Samuel Borges Photography/Shutterstock for page 57 bottom / Carlos Amarillo/
Shutterstock for page 63 top / Tomwang112/© iStock for page 65 middle / Syda Productions/© iStock for page 66 middle / Rawpixel.
com/Shutterstock for page 67 bottom / Elnur/Shutterstock for page 68 middle / irin-k/Shutterstock for page 72 bottom / asiseeit/©
iStock for page 76 bottom / michaeljung/Shutterstock for page 78 top / Pressmaster/Shutterstock for page 83 middle / Geraint Lewis/
Alamy for page 90 middle / India Picture/Shutterstock for page 92 bottom / Ivan Ponomarev/Shutterstock for page 94 top / Amy
Johansson/Shutterstock for page 98 middle / fotyma/© iStock for page 98 bottom / elnavegante/Shutterstock for page 99 middle /
Vitalii Hulai/Shutterstock for page 100 middle / Elnur/Shutterstock for page 103 middle / Ross Strachan/Shutterstock for page 103
bottom / Firman Wahyudin/Shutterstock for page 104 middle / duncan1890/© iStock for page 106 bottom / jgolby/Shutterstock for
page 108 bottom / legenda/Shutterstock for page 109 bottom Alla Shcherbak/Shutterstock for page 110 middle / bikeriderlondon/
Shutterstock for page 112 bottom / Aneese/Shutterstock for page 114 bottom / Sergey Nivens/Shutterstock for page 115 bottom
/ Syda Productions/Shutterstock for page 117 bottom / Alain36/© iStock for page 122 middle / goodluz/Shutterstock for page 123
bottom / wavebreakmedia/Shutterstock for page 124 bottom / silvergull/Shutterstock for page 125 bottom / My Life Graphic/
Shutterstock for page 127 bottom

CONTENTS

PART ONE: THE BASICS

PART TWO: GCSE ENGLISH LANGUAGE

PART TWO: GCSE ENGLISH LANGUAGE

Chapter 6: GCSE English Language practice papers

PART THREE: GCSE ENGLISH LITERATURE

Chapter 7: The basics: Core Literature skills and effects

Chapter 8: Paper 1, Sections A and B: Shakespeare and the nineteenth-century novel

Chapter 9: Paper 2, Section A: Modern prose and drama

Chapter 10: Paper 2, Section B: Poetry from the AQA anthology

Chapter 11: Paper 2, Section C: Unseen poetry

Chapter 12: GCSE English Literature practice papers

THE ASSESSMENT OBJECTIVES

If you are studying the AQA course for GCSE English Language and English Literature, your work will be examined through the Assessment Objectives below.

ENGLISH LANGUAGE

AO1 to AO4 relate to the Reading sections of the exam, and AO5 and AO6 to the Writing sections:

AO1	• Identify and interpret explicit and implicit information and ideas. • Select and synthesise evidence from different texts.
AO2	Explain, comment on and analyse how writers use language and structure to achieve effects and influence readers, using relevant subject terminology to support their views.
AO3	Compare writers' ideas and perspectives, as well as how these are conveyed, across two or more texts.
AO4	Evaluate texts critically and support this with appropriate textual references.
AO5	• Communicate clearly, effectively and imaginatively, selecting and adapting tone, style and register for different forms, purposes and audiences. • Organise information and ideas, using structural and grammatical features to support coherence and cohesion of texts.
AO6	Use a range of vocabulary and sentence structures for clarity, purpose and effect, with accurate spelling and punctuation. (20% of total marks.)

ENGLISH LITERATURE

AO1	Read, understand and respond to texts. Students should be able to: • maintain a critical style and develop an informed personal response • use textual references, including quotations, to support and illustrate interpretations.
AO2	Analyse the language, form and structure used by a writer to create meanings and effects, using relevant subject terminology where appropriate.
AO3	Show understanding of the relationships between texts and the contexts in which they were written.
AO4	Use a range of vocabulary and sentence structures, for clarity, purpose and effect, with accurate spelling and punctuation.

Look out for the AO labels throughout this book to help keep you on track!

CHAPTER 1: The basics: Spelling, punctuation and grammar

GRAMMATICAL TERMS

HOW'S YOUR SPaG?

We all make mistakes with our spelling, punctuation and grammar, so this section is designed to help you avoid the most obvious ones. But what is your SPaG like to begin with?

❶ Here is one student's not very successful story opening. Can you identify the errors?

> We was all siting on the harbor wall washing the boats sale bye suddenly a cry went up man overbord someone called, there was a terrific crack I saw a huge wooden mast fall from a yot it crashes into the see near wear a man in a yellow lifejacket floundered around what I call, in disbelieve, thats my dad!

WORD CLASSES

In English there are eight main word classes. A word can belong to more than one word class, depending on how it is used. For example:

● *She spread out the **plan** on the table.* (noun)
● *I **plan** to leave tomorrow.* (verb)

The table below lists the word classes and some sub-classes, with examples.

Nouns		Pronouns	Verbs		Adjectives
common	proper		auxiliary	main	
hat	London	I	have	see	big
		who			

Adverbs	Determiners	Prepositions	Conjunctions	
			coordinating	subordinating
quickly	the	of	or	because

❷ Copy the table, then add the words below to the correct column. Some words belong in more than one column.

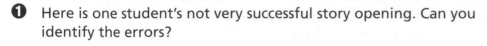

> while together table go himself his although happy you my/your to will a/an but on responsible may sharply and if in Saturday make tall Italy me soon April actor run book

DETERMINERS

When completing the table, you may have found it difficult to identify the **determiners**. Remember that a determiner shows a noun as **known** or **unknown**. For example, in the phrase 'this cat', the determiner 'this' refers to a specific, known cat.

Examples of determiners:

- Articles: 'the', 'a', 'an'
- Demonstratives: 'this', 'those'
- Possessives: 'my', 'your', 'his', 'her'
- Quantifiers: 'some', 'many'
- Certain question words: 'who', 'what'

MODIFIERS

When you modify something, you alter or adapt it. A **modifier** is not essential to a sentence, but it adds detail. It can make the meaning of a sentence more precise. For example, in the phrase 'the cream-cheese sandwich', 'sandwich' is modified by 'cream-cheese' to mean a particular type of sandwich. 'Cheese' is modified by 'cream' to mean a particular type of cheese.

> **TOP TIP**
> Remember, modifiers will make your writing more interesting.

❸ Modify the words 'teacher' and 'tea' to give more precise detail.

NOUN PHRASES

A **phrase** is a group of words that modifies a particular word, called the 'head'. A **noun phrase** is a phrase that has a noun as its head. For example:

- *Grey parrots can mimic.* 'Grey' modifies 'parrots', so 'grey' belongs to the noun phrase.
- *Most African grey parrots can mimic.* All the words in bold help to modify 'parrots', so they all belong to the noun phrase.

❹ Write down the noun phrases in these sentences. There may be more than one noun phrase in a sentence.
- *Uncle Ray's rabbit in the hutch is snoring.*
- *The small boy was a lost and bewildered newcomer.*

PREPOSITIONAL PHRASES

When **prepositional phrases** modify nouns they are adjectival, telling you which one, what type, how much or how many. For example: *The trees **by the river** sway gently.*

When prepositional phrases modify verbs they are **adverbial**. They tell you when, where, why or how. For example: *The river is flooding **because of the downpour.***

❺ Write down the prepositional phrases in these sentences. Note whether they are adjectival or adverbial phrases.
- *She's annoyed because of the holiday cancellation.*
- *It seems the robin on the windowsill visits daily.*

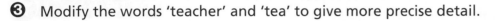

PROGRESS LOG [tick the correct box]   Needs more work ■   Getting there ■   Under control ■

SENTENCE CONSTRUCTION AND CLAUSES

Depending on their construction, sentences are described as simple, compound or complex. All sentences contain a subject and a verb. The subject is who or what the sentence is about. The verb tells you what the subject is doing, how it is feeling or its state.

SIMPLE SENTENCES

A **clause** is a group of words built around a verb as its head. A **simple sentence** has one **main clause** and it may contain an object as well as a subject and verb:

Leon   bought a guitar.

subject + verb + object

S   V   O

To find the object you can ask 'What?' So: 'Leon bought what?'

Sometimes a simple sentence may include an **indirect object**. To find this you could ask: 'Who or what received the direct object?'

Leon bought a guitar for Sally.

S   V   O   indirect object

You can add phrases to a simple sentence and vary their position.

Leon sang a ballad in the recording studio.

adverbial phrase

In the recording studio, Leon sang a ballad.

> **GET IT RIGHT!** ⭐
>
> A simple sentence does not need to have a direct object. It can just be a noun and a verb: 'Will sang.' 'He sang.' 'The boy sang.'

> **TOP TIP** ⭐
>
> You can use **minor sentences** to create a sense of urgency or emphasis, such as 'On my way!' The verb in minor sentences is usually implied rather than stated: 'I **am** on my way.'

COMPOUND SENTENCES

A **compound sentence** is made up of two independent clauses joined with a **coordinating conjunction**. Each of the independent clauses should make sense on its own. For example:

● *Rory turned his room upside down, **but** he couldn't find his mobile phone.*

● *Rory complained to his mother, **and** he shouted at his brother.*

❶ What type of sentences are these?
   ● *The snake slithered.*   ● *All in good time.*
   ● *Claire enjoys school, but she is always late for lessons.*

COMPLEX SENTENCES

A **complex sentence** usually has a main clause and a **subordinate clause**, which is dependent on the main clause to make sense. It can be connected by a **subordinating conjunction**:

*Niyusha loved Coco **because** he was a dog like no other.*

The subordinating conjunction shows the kind of link between the main clause and the subordinate one. 'Because' is a conjunction of **reason**.

A complex sentence can also be formed using a present or past **participle**:

> *Having agreed with the plan, Hannah had second thoughts.*

You could also say: *'Hannah, having agreed with the plan, had second thoughts.'* 'Having agreed with the plan' is a **non-finite clause** that does not make sense on its own. To form a full sentence, the participle and **non-finite verb** 'having' must be linked to a **finite verb**. In the example, 'had' is the finite verb.

'Lena played the drums' is a **finite clause** because it has a finite verb ('played'). Finite clauses have a verb in the past or present tense and make sense on their own.

- A **noun clause** is a subordinate clause that acts like a noun. It begins with words such as 'what', 'when', 'where', 'whether', 'whatever'. For example: *Whatever route you choose is fine with me.*
- A **relative clause** (sometimes known as an **adjectival clause**) is used to modify a noun or pronoun. It begins with a **relative pronoun** ('which', 'that', 'who', 'whose', 'whom') or sometimes a subordinating conjunction ('when' or 'where'). For example: *My neighbour, **who loves soccer**, never misses a match.*

TOP TIP

Non-finite clauses are useful because they can be placed in different parts of a sentence, adding variety to your writing.

ADVERBIAL CLAUSES

An **adverbial clause** functions as an **adverb**. It modifies the meaning of an **adjective**, verb or adverb. It asks a question: 'Why?', 'When?', 'Where?', 'How?', 'How much?', 'What condition?'

The adverbial clause is connected to the main clause by a subordinating conjunction, which comes at the beginning of the adverbial clause:

adverbial clause

Commercial and illegal logging must be controlled, if rainforests are to survive.

main clause

subordinating conjunction ('if')

❷ Find the adverbial clauses in these sentences:
- *Poor squatters cut down trees because they need money.*
- *In order to cultivate the coca plant, drug cartels use rainforest land.*
- *While tribespeople use rainforest resources, they take care of the forest.*

APPLYING YOUR SKILLS

❸ Combine these simple sentences to make complex ones. Use conjunctions and relative pronouns where you can.
- *Jake always ate well. He was a great chef. He cooked at home.*
- *Sian had a strong singing voice. She didn't practise enough. She had too much to do.*
- *Kai loved sky-diving. He had training. He finished work. He practised his skills.*

Remember:
- Vary the style of your sentences, i.e. dropping or replacing words, but you must keep the meaning!

PROGRESS LOG [tick the correct box]   Needs more work ☐   Getting there ☐   Under control ☐

SENTENCE TYPES AND TENSES

You can use four types of sentences to communicate your intentions:

- **Declarative:** Most sentences are declarative. They make a statement about someone/something: *'The mask was encrusted with fake diamonds.'*
- **Interrogative:** A question: *'Did you get the midday train?'*
- **Exclamatory:** Exclamatory sentences have an exclamation mark, which indicates strong feelings: *'The diamonds weren't real!'*
- **Imperative:** A command in which the subject (second person 'you', singular or plural) is left out: *'Try your best.'* (**'You** try your best.')

SUBJECT–VERB AGREEMENT

A singular subject in a sentence needs a singular verb. A plural subject needs a plural one. It is easy to make a mistake by wrongly identifying the subject:

- A **herd** of elephants **is** *thundering across the plain.* 'Herd' is the subject (not elephants) and there is only one herd.
- **Herds** of elephants **are** *thundering across the plain.* 'Herds' is the subject and there is more than one herd.

When used on their own in a sentence, 'either' and 'neither' are always the subject, so the verb must be singular:

- *Either of the two young footballers **is** ready to join the team.*
- *Neither of the singers **is** ready to perform yet.*

If you use 'either/or' and 'neither/nor', the subject nearest to the verb is the one that decides:

- *Neither the Farley twins nor **Jason has** won the prize.* (singular)
- *Either Jason or the **Farley twins have** won the prize.* (plural)

❶ Write a sentence in the present tense, using each of the following words as the subject: 'geese', 'book of rules', 'Kate or Jack', 'either of the acrobats', 'neither of the clowns'.

> **GET IT RIGHT!** ⭐
>
> A common mistake when using the verb 'to be' is to confuse 'was' and 'were':
>
> *You **was** late again!* **✗**
>
> *You **were** late again!* **✔**

TENSES

When you write about things that are **going** to happen, you need to use a present tense verb:

- *He **is** going on Tuesday.*

Many verbs follow similar spelling patterns when they change tenses or shift from singular to plural. For example:

- **Simple present tense:** 'I help', 'you help', 'he/she/it help**s**'
- **Simple past tense:** 'I help**ed**', 'you help**ed**', 'he/she/it help**ed**'

However, there are also many irregular verbs, such as the verb 'to be':

- **Simple present singular:** 'I am', 'you are', 'he/she/it is'
- **Simple present plural:** 'we are', 'you are', 'they are'
- **Simple past singular:** 'I was', 'you were', 'he/she/it was'
- **Simple past plural:** 'we were', 'you were', 'they were'

> **TOP TIP** ⭐
>
> Writers sometimes use the present tense to create particular effects, such as a strong sense of immediacy. For example, a story about a shipwreck might be more powerful written in the present tense than in the past tense.

The table below shows some irregular verbs in the third person singular.

Verb	Present third person singular	Past third person	Past participle
to blow	blows	blew	blown
to do	does	did	done
to draw	draws	drew	drawn
to eat	eats	ate	eaten
to fly	flies	flew	flown

THE ACTIVE AND THE PASSIVE

Verbs can be **active** or **passive**. In the active voice, the subject performs the action on the object:

Scruff	*ate*	*my homework.*
subject	**verb**	**object**

In the passive voice, the sentence is switched around. The active voice is more direct than the passive, but you might decide to use the passive if you want to focus on the item that is being acted on:

My homework	*was eaten*	*by Scruff.*
subject	**verb**	**agent**

❷ Change the following sentences to the passive. Decide whether or not you need to use 'by'.

- *The rapper performed a series of hits.*
- *She declared her intentions.*
- *Danny and Marlon anticipated the result.*

> **TOP TIP**
>
> Try to avoid using dialect or colloquialism unless you are using it for characterisation though voice or speech. Even then it should only be used very sparingly.

APPLYING YOUR SKILLS

❸ Rewrite this paragraph, correcting the subject–verb agreements and the tenses.

I were the first to get home on Wednesday, so I makes myself a cup of cappuccino with our new coffee maker. It do you good to relax sometimes. It weren't for long though, because five minutes later there were a loud banging on the door. When I opens it I sees my little brother stood there, sinking under the weight of his schoolbag, with tears streaming down his face.

Remember:

- A singular subject in a sentence needs a singular verb; a plural subject needs a plural verb.
- Do not confuse past and present tense.

PUNCTUATION

Punctuation is extremely important as it helps to give meaning to writing. If used incorrectly, it may confuse your reader.

COMMAS

A comma separates the **main clause** in a sentence from the **subordinate clause**:

> Bingley was by no means independent, but Darcy was clever.

> **independent (main) clause**   **subordinate clause**

A comma can also be used to separate items in a list or a series of descriptions:

> He was an odd mixture of light-heartedness and gloom, untidiness and fussiness, risk-taking and fear, so that even though she had lived with him for years, she felt she hardly knew him.

A comma should not be used to join two independent clauses (this is an error called a **comma splice**), because both clauses can stand on their own:

> Lottie turned the ignition to get the car going, the car remained silent.

Instead you should do one of the following:

- Replace the comma with a full stop and a capital letter: *Lottie turned the ignition to get the car going. The car remained silent.*

- Add a conjunction: *Lottie turned the ignition to get the car going,* **but** *the car remained silent.*

- Add a **semicolon**: *Lottie turned the ignition to get the car moving; the car remained silent.*

COLONS

A **colon** is used to indicate a pause. It has several functions.

It is used before lists:

> Beth waited discontentedly while Max dithered. Finally, Max drew up a list: tents, tent pegs, sleeping bags, water carrier, torch, ear plugs.

You can also use colons in play scripts to separate the name of the character from the words they speak:

> Arjun: Hurry up, we'll be late.

> Oli: Don't panic. I'm almost ready.

You can use colons to create impact in your writing. Look at this sentence:

> Horror is one thing you can be certain to find in a Gothic tale.

Withholding a word until the end of the sentence gives it emphasis, so a more dramatic way of saying this would be:

> There's one thing you can be certain to find in a Gothic tale: horror.

The clause before the colon is a main clause and can stand on its own.

GET IT RIGHT!

It is important to get basic punctuation right, as it can change the meaning of a sentence. What do these sentences mean with and without a comma?

- *Let's start baking, George!*
- *Let's start baking George!*

SEMICOLONS

A semicolon links two ideas, events or pieces of information:

Her difficulty in life was too little money; her comfort was good friendship.

Semicolons can also be used to separate items in a long list:

Giles always writes a lengthy list of travel items before he packs his holiday bag: toothbrush and toothpaste; floss; razor and shaving foam; shampoo; shower gel; soap; deodorant; corn plasters; insect repellent; bandages; blister pack; throat sweets and so on and so on!

DASHES

Dashes can be used to separate parts of a sentence, but they are mainly used for emphasis or additional explanation:

Help from strangers is not unusual – we see it daily.

BRACKETS

Round brackets ( ) are used to include extra information or an afterthought without altering the meaning of the sentence:

Beth waited discontentedly while Max dithered. Finally, Max drew up a list: tents, tent pegs (spare ones), sleeping bags, water carrier, torch, ear plugs (two pairs).

> **TOP TIP**
>
> **Square brackets [ ]** are often used to clarify or inform within a quoted text. For example: *Smith notes that 'she [Jane Austen] often depicted women whose lives depended on marriage for economic security'.*

ELLIPSES

Ellipses (a series of three dots) show where words have been deliberately left out. They can be used to create an effect, such as suspense:

At last the horse began to trot, but only to go round in circles so that Matt was at his wits' end, until the sound of galloping made him turn …

❶ Add at least fifty words to the following paragraph starter. Include a semicolon, a dash, brackets and ellipses.

Once he knew the contents of the letter, he left early – before dawn – choosing the fastest route. As he drove away …

> **TOP TIP**
>
> Ellipses and square brackets can also be used to show that words from a quoted text are missing: *As Smith comments, 'Charlotte Lucas in* Pride and Prejudice *is obliged to marry the ridiculous [...] Mr Collins'.*

DIRECT SPEECH

Direct speech refers to words that are actually spoken. They should be contained within speech marks. Direct speech also includes other punctuation features, which are shown on page 14.

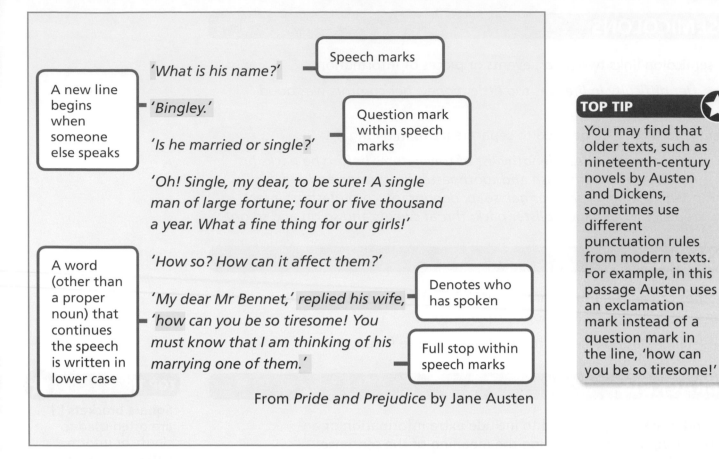

A new line begins when someone else speaks

'What is his name?'

Speech marks

'Bingley.'

'Is he married or single?'

Question mark within speech marks

'Oh! Single, my dear, to be sure! A single man of large fortune; four or five thousand a year. What a fine thing for our girls!'

'How so? How can it affect them?'

'My dear Mr Bennet,' replied his wife,

Denotes who has spoken

A word (other than a proper noun) that continues the speech is written in lower case

'how can you be so tiresome! You must know that I am thinking of his marrying one of them.'

Full stop within speech marks

From *Pride and Prejudice* by Jane Austen

REPORTED SPEECH

Reported speech is an **account** of what has been said. It does not show the actual words spoken, and no speech marks are used, but it should keep the meaning and the spirit of the words. Look at this example of reported speech based on the extract above. Note how tense and point of view change, as well as other features:

*Mrs Bennet replied **to her husband with some exasperation** that **he was** tiresome since he must know that **she intended Mr Bingley** to marry one of **their daughters**.*

APPLYING YOUR SKILLS ✔

❷   Read this example of direct speech from *Pride and Prejudice*. Change it into reported speech, using suitable punctuation, tense and point of view. You could begin: *Mr Bennet told his family that …*

'About a month ago I received this letter; and about a fortnight ago I answered it, for I thought it a case of some delicacy, and requiring early attention. It is from my cousin, Mr Collins, who, when I am dead, may turn you all out of this house as soon as he pleases.'

Remember:

● The tense and point of view will change.

● Read your finished paragraph to check that it is clear who or what is being referred to – for example, have you used suitable nouns?

PROGRESS LOG [tick the correct box]   Needs more work ◻   Getting there ◻   Under control ◻

PARAGRAPH ORGANISATION

Paragraphs give shape and structure to a piece of writing. They allow the reader to follow shifts in thinking.

SETTING OUT PARAGRAPHS

To indicate that you are beginning a new paragraph in your writing, you should indent the line:

> *Jimmy and his skateboard flew under the dilapidated railway bridge, along a series of concrete slabs made smooth by constant use. Skateboarding was Jimmy's main occupation.*
> *Usually, Tarik was with him, but today Jimmy was alone.*

A new paragraph should be used to indicate a change of idea, topic, place or time.

- Idea: ***However,*** *the theme of love is also important in …*
- Topic: ***In contrast,*** *Source A is focused on …*
- Place: ***Another*** *notorious place was the Clink …*
- Time: ***Meanwhile,*** *a great deal had changed.*

You should also use a new paragraph when a different person starts speaking (which is a rule of **direct speech**):

> *May looked disconcerted. 'But what have you done …'*
> *'With the key?' interrupted Jenny.*

CONNECTIVES

When you begin a new paragraph you can signal the change using **connectives**, which link paragraphs and show the relationship between them. The connectives in the examples above are shown in bold. The table below shows some common connectives and how to use them.

TOP TIP

The **topic sentence** does not have to be the first sentence in a paragraph. You can create a preliminary sentence first.

TOP TIP

A paragraph can be any length. It can even be a single sentence if you want to create impact by setting a statement or question apart from the rest of the text.

TOP TIP

It is easy to fall into the habit of over-using certain connectives, such as 'then'. Try to use a variety of connectives in your writing.

Addition of ideas	Order or sequence	Examples	Cause and effect
In addition	Firstly	For example	Consequently
As well as	Secondly	For instance	As a result
Besides	Next	Such as	Since
Also	Later	As can be seen	Because

Compare & contrast	Qualify	Purpose	Sum up
Similarly	However	To this end	Finally
In the same way	Still	For this purpose	To sum up
In contrast	Yet	For this reason	In conclusion
On the other hand	Having said that	In order to	

APPLYING YOUR SKILLS

1 Find the start of new paragraphs in this report:

Exceptionally heavy rain over a prolonged period this morning caused flash floods and brought disruption to several areas in the West Midlands. Flood warnings were issued yesterday. Roads have been inundated and transport is at a standstill. Those most affected are to the south of Birmingham. In addition, rail and property has been affected. There are unconfirmed reports that lines have been closed in the South East. There are no reports of injury or major damage to property, but five hundred homes are without power. Three schools are closed. Finally, heavy rain is expected to continue today and tomorrow moving eastwards. The environment agency has issued further flood warnings.

Remember:

● Read the text through with expression to check you have started the new paragraph in the right place.

PROGRESS LOG [tick the correct box]   Needs more work ▮   Getting there ▮   Under control ▮

SPELLING   (A06) (A04)

You do not always spell English words as they sound, but there are some useful spelling rules that can help you remember how to spell certain words.

PLURALS

When you add 's' to nouns that end in 'y', change 'y' to 'ie' when there is a consonant before the 'y':

> *lorry → lorries   cherry → cherries   memory → memories*

If there is a vowel before the 'y', just add 's':

> *donkey → donkeys   journey → journeys   tray → trays*

Add 'es' to nouns that end in '-ch', '-s', '-sh', '-x', '-z':

> *peach → peaches   glass → glasses   wish → wishes   fox → foxes*
> *buzz → buzzes*

(Exception: *stomach → stomachs*)

Nouns ending in 'f' or 'fe' often change to 'v' when 'es' is added:

> *wolf → wolves   knife → knives*

For most nouns that end in 'ff' or have two vowels before 'f', just add 's': 'cuffs', 'chiefs'.

PREFIXES AND SUFFIXES

Prefixes that end in a vowel do not change when added to a word. However, remember that double letters can occur.

ante → antenatal   un → un**n**ecessary

semi → semicircle   mis → mi**ss**pell

pre → premeditate   ir → ir**r**egular

When you add a **suffix** beginning with a vowel to a word that ends in a silent 'e', you usually drop the 'e'. However, if the word ends in 'ce' or 'ge' you keep the 'e'.

adventure → adventur**ous**   notice → notic**eable**

excite → excit**able**   manage → manag**eable**

When you add 'all', 'full' or 'till' to a word, drop the second 'l':

all → also, always, almost   full → hopeful, fulfill   till → until

❶ Look at the following words. Which ones are spelt incorrectly? Are there any exceptions? Which are literary terms?

> quays heros countrys sniffs vallies librarys loaves
> parodies rooves quizzes motifs ironies dreadfull
> misunderstood paradoxes irigation reversible outrageous
> ambiguities advantagous misspoken

> **TOP TIP**
>
> Suffixes and prefixes build words, change meaning and can help to extend your vocabulary. They also change word classes. For example, adding 'ance' to the adjective 'resist' turns it into the noun 'resistance'.

HOMOPHONES

Words that sound the same but that mean different things are called **homophones**. There are many homophones and it is easy to make mistakes. Look at these homophones:

- **its** = shows belonging; **it's** = shortened form of 'it is'
- **their** = belonging to them; **there** = that place; **they're** = shortened form of 'they are'
- **whose** = belonging to someone; **who's** = shortened form of 'who is'

❷ Look at the following homophones. Copy down any that you confuse in your writing. Look up their meanings to help you remember the different spellings.

> to, two, too   fair, fare   hare, hair   right, rite, write, wright
> weather, whether   aloud, allowed   accept, except   missed, mist
> stationary, stationery   principal, principle

> **TOP TIP**
>
> Create your own spelling notebook A–Z. Record any words you are unsure of, particularly homophones.

IMPROVING YOUR SPELLING

Try recording a word with a similar pattern as a prompt:

Correct word	Reminder
mem**ento**	**member**
toma**toes**	**toes**

Or, you can split complex words into sound sections that help visualise the spelling. Say each word out loud and listen to its rhythm to help you remember:

a-cco-mmo-date   di-le-mma   a-ppear-ance   def-in-ite-ly

Mnemonics are phrases used as memory aids. For example, you can create a nonsense phrase to remind you how to spell a word or name:

Word	Phrase reminder
ochre	**O**nly **c**arrots **h**ave **r**adar **e**yes.
Arctic	**A**ll **r**abbits **c**an **t**alk **i**n **c**ode.

APPLYING YOUR SKILLS

❸ Identify the spelling errors in this paragraph. How many are homophones? Which **homophones** are spelled correctly?

Loseing no time, he grabbed two peices of the tough, fibreous rope and tide them together with a complex not I had never scene before. He pulled the join untill it was tight enough not to brake. With one quick move he through it towards the stout branch above us. It missed. He threw it hire. It missed again.

Remember:

● You should recognise an error quickly; if you are unsure, leave it as it is.
● Record the correct spellings of any errors you did not identify.

PROGRESS CHECK FOR CHAPTER 1

GOOD PROGRESS

I can:
● Use different types of sentences to create effects ☐
● Use different types of sentences that are mostly grammatically correct ☐
● Use a range of punctuation successfully most of the time ☐
● Spell most words correctly including complex words and use an increasingly wide range of vocabulary ☐

EXCELLENT PROGRESS

I can:
● Use the full range of sentence types to create a variety of effects ☐
● Use a range of sentences including complex structures and to a high level of grammatical accuracy ☐
● Use different kinds of punctuation to create effects, and rarely make errors ☐
● Spell accurately to a high level and use an ambitious range of vocabulary ☐

CHAPTER 2: Paper 1, Section A: Reading fiction

WHAT'S IT ALL ABOUT?

In Paper 1, Section A, of your English Language exam you will answer four questions based on an extract from a modern novel (twentieth or twenty-first century), referred to as 'the source'.

TIMING AND APPROACH

You should spend about an hour on Section A, including up to fifteen minutes carefully reading the extract. You may find it helpful to read the extract once, then read the questions, then return to the extract and read it again, annotating it to help you answer the questions.

Each question will direct you to focus on a particular part of the extract, so another possible approach is to read the extract once, then read the questions, then reread and annotate the extract for each question in turn as you answer it.

> **TOP TIP** ★
>
> There are no marks for spelling, punctuation or grammar in Paper 1, Section A. However, if you express yourself clearly and accurately it will be easier for the examiner to understand your answers and credit you for them.

EARNING THE MARKS

There are 80 marks for the whole of Paper 1, and 40 marks are for Section A. The table below shows how these are allocated and gives an overview of what you need to do for each question.

PAPER 1, SECTION A

Question	Marks	What you must do
1	4	List four relevant facts from the extract, such as what the weather is.
2	8	Explain and analyse how the writer uses language for a particular purpose.
3	8	Analyse how the whole extract is structured.
4	20	Evaluate how well the writer has created a particular impression of some aspect of the text, such as character, setting or atmosphere. You will also be expected to give a personal response to the text – saying what you feel about it and why, supporting your ideas with evidence.

For Question 1, you simply have to list the facts. For Questions 2, 3 and 4 you need to support your claims with evidence and analysis.

FINDING EXPLICIT INFORMATION

WHAT IS EXPLICIT INFORMATION AND HOW DO YOU IDENTIFY IT?

PAPER 1,
SECTION A, Q1

The simplest kind of information in a text is **explicit** information. This means information that is stated as fact. For example:

> *The bus stop was 200 metres away. Emily sprinted desperately towards it.*

The most obvious fact here is 'The bus stop was 200 metres away.' This is stated explicitly. You might guess that Emily wants to catch the bus, but that is not stated explicitly.

The exam question will direct you to a section of the text, like this:

> *Read again the first part of the source, lines 1–10. List **four** things from this part of the text about Emily's daily routine.*

Make sure you focus on the correct section. Underline or circle four facts in the extract, then list them.

> ⭐ **GET IT RIGHT!**
>
> There are only 4 marks for this question – you will not earn more by listing more than four details. Also remember that you are being asked to list facts, not give your opinion.

❶ Read this story opening. What explicit information can you find in it?

It was a hot afternoon, and the railway carriage was correspondingly sultry[1], and the next stop was at Templecombe, nearly an hour ahead. The occupants of the carriage were a small girl, and a smaller girl, and a small boy. An aunt belonging to the children occupied one corner seat, and the further corner seat on the opposite side was occupied by a bachelor who was a stranger to their party, but the small girls and the small boy emphatically[2] occupied the compartment. Both the aunt and the children were conversational in a limited, persistent way, reminding one of the attentions of a housefly that refused to be discouraged. Most of the aunt's remarks seemed to begin with 'Don't.' and nearly all of the children's remarks began with 'Why?' The bachelor said nothing out loud.

From 'The Storyteller' by Saki (H. H. Munro)

sultry[1] – hot and humid
emphatically[2] – very definitely

❷ Why would it be incorrect to write *'The children and their aunt are going to Templecombe'*?

The table below shows some irregular verbs in the third person singular.

Verb	Present third person singular	Past third person	Past participle
to blow	blows	blew	blown
to do	does	did	done
to draw	draws	drew	drawn
to eat	eats	ate	eaten
to fly	flies	flew	flown

THE ACTIVE AND THE PASSIVE

Verbs can be **active** or **passive**. In the active voice, the subject performs the action on the object:

Scruff   *ate*   *my homework.*

subject   **verb**   **object**

In the passive voice, the sentence is switched around. The active voice is more direct than the passive, but you might decide to use the passive if you want to focus on the item that is being acted on:

My homework was eaten by Scruff.

subject   **verb**   **agent**

❷   Change the following sentences to the passive. Decide whether or not you need to use 'by'.

- *The rapper performed a series of hits.*
- *She declared her intentions.*
- *Danny and Marlon anticipated the result.*

> **TOP TIP**
>
> Try to avoid using dialect or colloquialism unless you are using it for characterisation though voice or speech. Even then it should only be used very sparingly.

APPLYING YOUR SKILLS

❸   Rewrite this paragraph, correcting the subject–verb agreements and the tenses.

I were the first to get home on Wednesday, so I makes myself a cup of cappuccino with our new coffee maker. It do you good to relax sometimes. It weren't for long though, because five minutes later there were a loud banging on the door. When I opens it I sees my little brother stood there, sinking under the weight of his schoolbag, with tears streaming down his face.

Remember:

- A singular subject in a sentence needs a singular verb; a plural subject needs a plural verb.
- Do not confuse past and present tense.

PROGRESS LOG [tick the correct box]   Needs more work ☐   Getting there ☐   Under control ☐

PUNCTUATION

Punctuation is extremely important as it helps to give meaning to writing. If used incorrectly, it may confuse your reader.

COMMAS

A comma separates the **main clause** in a sentence from the **subordinate clause**:

> *Bingley was by no means independent, but Darcy was clever.*

> **independent (main) clause**   **subordinate clause**

A comma can also be used to separate items in a list or a series of descriptions:

> *He was an odd mixture of light-heartedness and gloom, untidiness and fussiness, risk-taking and fear, so that even though she had lived with him for years, she felt she hardly knew him.*

A comma should not be used to join two independent clauses (this is an error called a **comma splice**), because both clauses can stand on their own:

> *Lottie turned the ignition to get the car going, the car remained silent.*

Instead you should do one of the following:

- Replace the comma with a full stop and a capital letter: *Lottie turned the ignition to get the car going. The car remained silent.*

- Add a conjunction: *Lottie turned the ignition to get the car going,* **but** *the car remained silent.*

- Add a **semicolon**: *Lottie turned the ignition to get the car moving; the car remained silent.*

COLONS

A **colon** is used to indicate a pause. It has several functions.

It is used before lists:

> *Beth waited discontentedly while Max dithered. Finally, Max drew up a list: tents, tent pegs, sleeping bags, water carrier, torch, ear plugs.*

You can also use colons in play scripts to separate the name of the character from the words they speak:

> *Arjun: Hurry up, we'll be late.*

> *Oli: Don't panic. I'm almost ready.*

You can use colons to create impact in your writing. Look at this sentence:

> *Horror is one thing you can be certain to find in a Gothic tale.*

Withholding a word until the end of the sentence gives it emphasis, so a more dramatic way of saying this would be:

> *There's one thing you can be certain to find in a Gothic tale: horror.*

The clause before the colon is a main clause and can stand on its own.

> **GET IT RIGHT!**
>
> It is important to get basic punctuation right, as it can change the meaning of a sentence. What do these sentences mean with and without a comma?
>
> - *Let's start baking, George!*
> - *Let's start baking George!*

EXAM FOCUS

Below are six points that a student might make about the extract. Look at the comments about each point:

1 'It was a hot afternoon.'

1. Correct – you can make short quotes from the text if the meaning is clear

2 There are five people in the compartment.

2. Correct – a simple sum

3 There is a fly in the compartment.

3. Incorrect – the conversation is compared with a fly

4 The children and their aunt speak to each other often.

4. Correct – 'persistent'

5 The children ask many questions.

5. Correct – 'Why?'

6 The bachelor is irritated by the children.

6. May turn out to be true – we cannot be sure yet

APPLYING YOUR SKILLS

❸ Read this further extract from 'The Storyteller' and list four pieces of explicit information.

The child moved reluctantly to the window. 'Why are those sheep being driven out of that field?' he asked.

'I expect they are being driven to another field where there is more grass,' said the aunt weakly.

'But there is lots of grass in that field,' protested the boy; 'there's nothing else but grass there. Aunt, there's lots of grass in that field.'

'Perhaps the grass in the other field is better,' suggested the aunt fatuously.[1]

'Why is it better?' came the swift, inevitable question.

'Oh, look at those cows!' exclaimed the aunt. Nearly every field along the line had contained cows or bullocks, but she spoke as though she were drawing attention to a rarity.

'Why is the grass in the other field better?' persisted Cyril.

The frown on the bachelor's face was deepening to a scowl. He was a hard, unsympathetic man, the aunt decided in her mind.

fatuously[1] – stupidly, pointlessly

Remember:

- Only list points that are definitely correct.
- Do not mistake a character's opinion for a fact.

FINDING IMPLICIT INFORMATION

WHAT IS IMPLICIT INFORMATION AND HOW DO YOU IDENTIFY IT?

A01

PAPER 1,
SECTION A, Q1

Writers may imply information, suggesting or hinting at it with description or word choices rather than stating it explicitly. Identifying **implicit** information is a key skill in English Language and Literature. Consider these lines:

- *Sam's face was turning purple. His knuckles were clenched and white.*
- *Sam was furious.*

Most readers would find the first version more interesting and enjoy **inferring** (deducing) the implied information that is stated explicitly in the second version. They would identify the signs that Sam is furious.

Read this continuation of 'The Storyteller' and think about this question: 'What does the writer **imply** about the characters?'

The smaller girl created a diversion by beginning to recite 'On the Road to Mandalay'.[1] She only knew the first line, but she put her limited knowledge to the fullest possible use. She repeated the line over and over again in a dreamy but resolute and very audible voice; it seemed to the bachelor as though someone had had a bet with her that she could not repeat the line aloud two thousand times without stopping. Whoever it was who had made the wager was likely to lose his bet.

  'Come over here and listen to a story,' said the aunt, when the bachelor had looked twice at her and once at the communication cord.[2]

From 'The Storyteller' by Saki (H. H. Munro)

'On the Road to Mandalay'[1] – a poem by Rudyard Kipling
communication cord[2] – a way for passengers to let a train driver know if there is an emergency

---

How would you approach this question?

- The question says 'characters' (plural), so try to find information about all three characters.
- Look only for **implied** information.

The table below shows some implied information and evidence.

Character	Implied information	Evidence
Girl	She is determined to keep repeating the line.	'resolute'
Bachelor	He is exasperated by the children, especially the girl.	It seems as if she will keep repeating the line 'two thousand times'. This hints at his exasperation by exaggerating his fears.
Aunt	She feels she ought to stop the children irritating the bachelor.	She decides to tell them a story after the bachelor 'looked twice at her and once at the communication cord'. This hints that he might pull the emergency cord rather than have to listen to the girl.

❶ What other implied information can you find about the girl – for example, in the writer's choice of the phrase 'created a diversion'?

❷ What could be implied about the bachelor by the particular way in which the writer hints at the man's worries about the girl?

TOP TIP

When giving implied information, add a *short* quotation or explanation to support your point.

EXAM FOCUS

Here are three further points that a student thinks are implied in the extract. Look at the comments about each point:

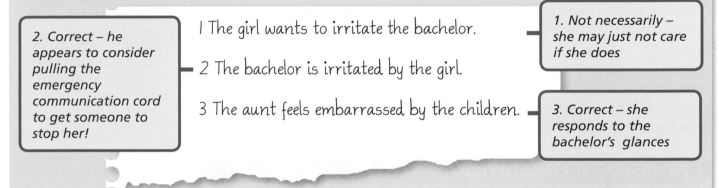

2. Correct – he appears to consider pulling the emergency communication cord to get someone to stop her!

1 The girl wants to irritate the bachelor.

2 The bachelor is irritated by the girl.

3 The aunt feels embarrassed by the children.

1. Not necessarily – she may just not care if she does

3. Correct – she responds to the bachelor's glances

APPLYING YOUR SKILLS

❸ Read this further extract from the story. Find four pieces of implied information about the characters.

The children moved listlessly towards the aunt's end of the carriage. Evidently her reputation as a storyteller did not rank high in their estimation.

In a low, confidential voice, interrupted at frequent intervals by loud, petulant questions from her listeners, she began an un-enterprising and deplorably uninteresting story about a little girl who was good, and made friends with everyone on account of her goodness, and was finally saved from a mad bull by a number of rescuers who admired her moral character.

'Wouldn't they have saved her if she hadn't been good?' demanded the bigger of the small girls. It was exactly the question that the bachelor had wanted to ask.

Remember:

● Look for information about **all** the characters.

● Look for clues in description and word choices.

● A writer's word choices may imply information.

QUOTING OR PARAPHRASING EFFECTIVELY

HOW CAN YOU QUOTE OR PARAPHRASE A TEXT EFFECTIVELY TO SUPPORT YOUR POINTS?

PAPER 1,
SECTION A,
Q1, 2 AND 4

In all your English exams, you should give evidence and support your comments on a text by quoting or paraphrasing.

- **Quoting** means giving the exact words used, in quotation marks. You should quote if the exact word choice is important.
- **Paraphrasing** means putting information into your own words. It is useful to show you **understand** the text and to make your response more **concise**.

In Paper 1, Section A, Question 1 you might quote a simple statement without explaining it. If you are referring to implied information, give a short quotation (it can even be one word) to support your point. In other parts of the exam, you will need to explain the significance of your quotation or paraphrase.

TOP TIP

Select your evidence carefully. If there are several possible quotations you could use to make a point, choose the best one or two.

CHOOSING A QUOTATION

Read the extract below, then answer the question that follows.

> She was a tall woman of imperious mien,[1] handsome, with definite black eyebrows. Her smooth black hair was parted exactly. For a few moments she stood steadily watching the miners as they passed along the railway: then she turned towards the brook course. Her face was calm and set, her mouth was closed with disillusionment. After a moment she called:
>   'John!' There was no answer. She waited, and then said distinctly: 'Where are you?'
>   'Here!' replied a child's sulky voice from among the bushes. The woman looked piercingly through the dusk.
>   'Are you at that brook?' she asked sternly.
>   For answer the child showed himself before the raspberry-canes that rose like whips. He was a small, sturdy boy of five. He stood quite still, defiantly.
>
> From 'The Odour of Chrysanthemums' by D. H. Lawrence
>
> *imperious mien*[1] – a commanding appearance

❶ What words or phrases describing the woman's appearance suggest:
- A strong, decisive character?
- That she has some reason to be unhappy?

PRESENTING QUOTATIONS

Suppose you want to quote an **adverb** to show that the woman in the extract is a firm parent. You might say:

● *She is a strict parent: 'she asked sternly'. The adverb shows ...*
● *She is strict with her boy ('she asked sternly') and expects him to ...*
● *She speaks to her son 'sternly' when she suspects that he ...*

Any of these is acceptable. However, the third method is often the most effective – **embedding** the quotation. Use this at least some of the time, as it will make your writing more fluent. Always remember to use quotation marks around words or phrases that are taken directly from the text.

❷ Write two sentences commenting on the character of the mother in the extract above, embedding the following quotations:
● *'distinctly'*
● *'piercingly'*

> **GET IT RIGHT!**
>
> When embedding a quotation, always make sure the sentence works grammatically with the embedded word or phrase.

PARAPHRASING

Use paraphrasing when it is a detail or character action in the text that is important rather than the author's word choice.

EXAM FOCUS

Read this paragraph in which a student has quoted from a text and paraphrased where necessary. Some of its features have been highlighted:

> The woman's 'hair ... parted exactly' suggests that she is decisive and takes care with her appearance. She demands to know where her son is, speaking 'distinctly' so that he has no excuse for not answering her. She looks 'piercingly' into the gloom, suggesting that she is determined to find her son, and that he cannot hide from her.

Paraphrase

Explains the significance of the adverb choice

*Embedded quotation with **ellipsis** (...) to preserve the sentence's grammar*

Embedded quotation; paraphrase of 'through the dusk' helps to explain

APPLYING YOUR SKILLS

❸ Write two sentences showing what you learn about the boy in this extract.
Remember:

● In the first sentence, paraphrase the **explicit** information about the boy.
● In the second, use an embedded quotation to analyse his responses to his mother.

PROGRESS LOG [tick the correct box]   Needs more work ☐   Getting there ☐   Under control ☐

ANALYSING LANGUAGE FEATURES AND EFFECTS

HOW DOES THE CHOICE OF PARTICULAR WORDS AND PHRASES CREATE EFFECTS?

A02

PAPER 1,
SECTION A, Q2

Writers use language in different ways for different purposes. For example, they may want to create a striking image, suggest a hidden meaning or build tension.

Read the extract below. How does the writer use **words and phrases** to show that Yvette is in danger?

> *She* [Yvette] *heard somebody shouting, and looked round. Down the path through the larch trees the gipsy was bounding. The gardener, away beyond, was also running. Simultaneously she became aware of a great roar, which, before she could move, accumulated to a vast deafening snarl. The gipsy was gesticulating. She looked round, behind her.*
>
> From *The Virgin and the Gipsy* by D. H. Lawrence

How would you answer the question?

- First, decide what the **focus of the question** is – 'that Yvette is in danger'.
- **Choose examples** of **words and phrases** that help to show danger.
- Select the **most appropriate ones** and **use correct grammatical terms**.
- **Describe the effects**.

The table below describes two examples from the text.

TOP TIP

Only use literary terms if you are sure of them. You will still get credit for selecting words and describing their effects.

Signs of danger	Words/phrases	Terms (where useful)	Effect
The gipsy is running towards Yvette.	*was bounding*	Verb (past continuous)	Powerful verb emphasises gipsy's sense of urgency. Use of continuous verb suggests that the gipsy is in the background, some distance from Yvette.
Yvette's attention is drawn in two directions at once.	*Simultaneously*	Conjunctive **adverb**	Points out Yvette's sudden awareness of danger. Heightens tension further.

EXAM FOCUS

Read the start of this successful response to the question. Some of its qualities have been highlighted:

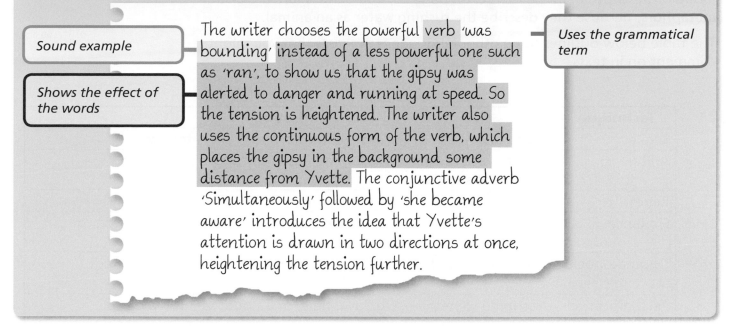

Sound example

Shows the effect of the words

The writer chooses the powerful verb 'was bounding' instead of a less powerful one such as 'ran', to show us that the gipsy was alerted to danger and running at speed. So the tension is heightened. The writer also uses the continuous form of the verb, which places the gipsy in the background some distance from Yvette. The conjunctive adverb 'Simultaneously' followed by 'she became aware' introduces the idea that Yvette's attention is drawn in two directions at once, heightening the tension further.

Uses the grammatical term

What mistakes **might** a student have made in answering this question?

- They might have commented on the sentence structure – not asked for here.
- They might have focused on the landscape instead of the danger.
- They might have mentioned the effects but not shown how they were created (the evidence).
- They might have identified the types of phrases or words incorrectly.

Reread the extract at the top of page 26, then answer these two questions:

❶ What **verbs**, **nouns** and **adjectives** best show that Yvette is in danger?

❷ Describe their **effects**.

NOW YOU TRY IT

Read this further extract from earlier in the text, then answer the question below.

> *And she felt too lazy, too lazy, too lazy. She strayed in the garden by the river, half dreamy, expecting something. While the gleam of spring sun lasted, she would be out of doors. Indoors Granny, sitting back like some awful old prelate,[1] in her bulk of black silk and her white lace cap, was warming her feet by the fire …*

prelate[1] – a high-ranking clergyman, such as a bishop

❸ How does the writer use words and phrases to describe Yvette's feelings of idleness?
Remember:

- Stick to the focus of the question.
- Mention words and phrases.
- Describe their effects.

CHOOSING TECHNIQUES TO CREATE EFFECTS

Sometimes writers use specific language techniques to create a particular mood or description. In the extract on page 26, 'roar' and 'snarl' are also **metaphors**, because they describe the rushing water as an animal.

The table below outlines some other language techniques that you might comment on in texts.

Technique	Definition
Simile	a comparison using 'like', 'as' or 'than': 'a face like a tomato'
Alliteration	repeated use of consonant sounds, especially at the start of words, as in 'dirty, dark and damp'
Repetition	words or phrases used more than once, for emphasis
Sibilance	strongly stressed consonants making a 'hissing' sound, e.g. 'whisper of silvery snow'
Onomatopoeia	words that sound like the thing they describe, such as 'Crash! Thud!'
Personification	describing something, e.g. love, time, or a flood, as if it is a person

Read this further extract from *The Virgin and the Gipsy*. Which of the **techniques** in the table above does the writer use to describe Yvette's desperate circumstances?

> *Yvette was blind to everything but the stairs. Blind, unconscious of everything save the steps rising beyond the water, she clambered up like a wet, shuddering cat, in a state of unconsciousness. It was not till she was on the landing, dripping and shuddering till she could not stand erect, clinging to the banisters, while the house shook and the water raved below, that she was aware of the sodden gipsy.*

How would you approach this question?

- Decide what its **focus** is – 'Yvette's desperate circumstances'.
- Find **examples** of Yvette's desperate circumstances and sum them up in your own words.
- Select the **most appropriate ones** and identify the **techniques** used.
- Describe the **effects**.

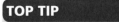

TOP TIP

Look for techniques that appeal to a range of senses, not only sight.

EXAM FOCUS

Read the start of this successful response to the question. Some of its qualities have been highlighted:

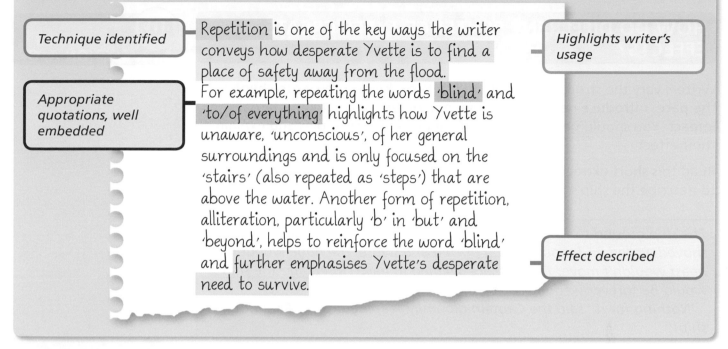

Technique identified

Appropriate quotations, well embedded

Repetition is one of the key ways the writer conveys how desperate Yvette is to find a place of safety away from the flood. For example, repeating the words 'blind' and 'to/of everything' highlights how Yvette is unaware, 'unconscious', of her general surroundings and is only focused on the 'stairs' (also repeated as 'steps') that are above the water. Another form of repetition, alliteration, particularly 'b' in 'but' and 'beyond', helps to reinforce the word 'blind' and further emphasises Yvette's desperate need to survive.

Highlights writer's usage

Effect described

Reread the extract on page 28 and answer these questions:

❹ Find **two other techniques** in the extract.

❺ Describe their **effects**.

APPLYING YOUR SKILLS

Read this extract from later in the text, then use what you have learned about the effect of language choices (words, phrases and techniques) to answer the question below.

The bridge was gone. But the flood had abated, and the house, that leaned forwards as if it were making a stiff bow to the stream, stood now in mud and wreckage, with a great heap of fallen masonry and debris at the south-west corner. Awful were the gaping mouths of rooms!

❻ How does the writer use language to describe what has happened to the house?

Remember:

- Stick to the focus of the question.
- Mention words and phrases.
- Describe their effects.

ANALYSING THE EFFECTS OF DIFFERENT TYPES OF SENTENCES

HOW DO DIFFERENT SENTENCE TYPES CREATE EFFECTS?

PAPER 1, SECTION A, Q2

Writers vary the structure, length and style of their sentences to change the pace, introduce new information, add details or create emotional impact. You should be able to identify appropriate examples and explain their effect.

Read this short extract. How does the writer use **different sentence forms** to describe the ship's predicament?

> *The ship ground to a halt. Although the sailors on the ice pushed and shoved, yelled and shouted, and puffed and swore, the huge wooden beast wouldn't move. The pack ice seemed to have closed and the ship would be forever wedded to it.*
>
> *'Nothing for it,' said the Captain gloomily, leaping down. 'Abandon ship!'*

How would you approach this sort of question?

- Decide what the **focus of the question** is – 'the ship's predicament' (the problem it faces).
- Find **examples** of the problem being described.
- Select the **most appropriate evidence** and identify the **sentence forms**.
- Describe the **effects**.

Look back at pages 10–11 to remind yourself of the different sentence forms writers use to add variety and create effects in their work. The table below describes two examples of sentence forms from the text.

> **TOP TIP**
>
> This will probably only be one part of a question worth 8 marks (so 2–3 marks for this part), so although there are four stages here, you would need to do this very quickly in your head, or in brief notes.

Problem	Example	Sentence form	Effect
The ship meets trouble.	*The ship ground to a halt.*	Simple sentence	Suggests the abrupt, sudden nature of the moment.
The sailors try everything but cannot move it.	*Although the sailors on the ice pushed and shoved, yelled and shouted, and puffed and swore, the huge wooden beast wouldn't move.*	Complex sentence	The long subordinated sentence suggests all the men's efforts.

EXAM FOCUS

Read this successful response to the question. Some of its qualities have been highlighted:

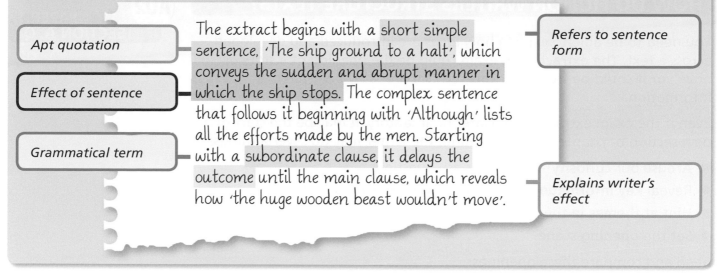

Apt quotation

Effect of sentence

Grammatical term

The extract begins with a short simple sentence, 'The ship ground to a halt', which conveys the sudden and abrupt manner in which the ship stops. The complex sentence that follows it beginning with 'Although' lists all the efforts made by the men. Starting with a subordinate clause, it delays the outcome until the main clause, which reveals how 'the huge wooden beast wouldn't move'.

Refers to sentence form

Explains writer's effect

What mistakes **might** a student have made in answering this question?

● They might have commented on the Captain's feelings – not asked for here.
● They might have mentioned the different forms but not mentioned the effects.
● They might have mentioned the effects but not specified the types of sentences used.
● They might have commented on vocabulary and not mentioned sentences at all.

Reread the extract on page 30, then answer these two questions:

❶ What two other sentence forms or styles are used in the extract?

❷ How do they contribute to the effect?

APPLYING YOUR SKILLS

Read this further extract from the same text, then answer the question below.

It was just before nightfall that it happened. Although the men had posted guards on all sides of the camp, somehow they must have missed its approach. Grabbing rifles and throwing off blankets, the men leapt into action. A flare went up. There it was! A huge, lumbering white monster appeared out of the gloom. It was a polar bear.

❸ How does the writer use sentence forms to describe the drama of the polar bear's attack?

Remember:

● Stick to the focus of the question.
● Mention the sentence forms.
● Describe their effects.

ANALYSING THE STRUCTURE OF A TEXT

HOW DO FICTION WRITERS STRUCTURE TEXTS?

PAPER 1,
SECTION A, Q3

You need to be able to explain how ideas are introduced and developed across a text. The extract in an exam could be the opening of a story or novel, or it could be from later on. You will probably be given this information.

Even if the exam extract is from later on in a story, it may be the start of a new section or chapter. In any opening, the writer may do several things:

- Arouse our **curiosity** – making us ask questions
- Reveal **key information** about characters and their situation
- Hint at **themes** in the story
- Set the **opening scene**

Read and compare these openings:

A *None of them knew the colour of the sky. Their eyes glanced level, and were fastened upon the waves that swept toward them. These waves were of the hue of slate, save for the tops, which were of foaming white, and all of the men knew the colours of the sea.*

From 'The Open Boat' by Stephen Crane

B *There was no possibility of taking a walk that day. We had been wandering, indeed, in the leafless shrubbery an hour in the morning; but since dinner (Mrs Reed, when there was no company, dined early) the cold winter wind had brought with it clouds so sombre, and a rain so penetrating, that further out-door exercise was now out of the question.*

From *Jane Eyre* by Charlotte Brontë

C *It is a truth universally acknowledged, that a single man in possession of a good fortune, must be in want of a wife.*

From *Pride and Prejudice* by Jane Austen

---

❶ What is revealed or suggested in each opening?

❷ What questions does each opening raise?

TOP TIP ⭐

Look for how a text engages the reader. For example, opening A gets our attention with a puzzling statement that becomes clearer when we realise the men are concentrating on the rough sea. We ask ourselves why this is so.

EXAM FOCUS

Read this extract from a response to a question based on opening **B**.
Some of its qualities have been highlighted:

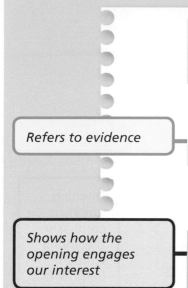

The opening makes us wonder why a walk is impossible, and then explains, providing a surprising amount of information. It moves from morning to afternoon through 'that day' in the narrator's memory when they had little to do, as shown by their 'wandering' on a cold winter's day. It reveals the time of day, the season and the weather. It also introduces 'Mrs Reed' as someone who decides what time lunch will be. The passage also raises questions: who Mrs Reed is, who the narrator is and why she is wandering about. Finally, the 'sombre' weather creates a gloomy mood.

> **Identifies the 'question and answer' format**

> **Refers to evidence**

> **Shows how the opening engages our interest**

The student does not make the mistake of trying to analyse words or sentences in detail, concentrating instead on what the opening achieves and how ideas are developed and structured.

NOW YOU TRY IT

Read the continuation of opening **B**, then answer the question below.

I was glad of it: I never liked long walks, especially on chilly afternoons: dreadful to me was the coming home in the raw twilight, with nipped fingers and toes, and a heart saddened by the chidings of Bessie, the nurse, and humbled by the consciousness of my physical inferiority to Eliza, John, and Georgiana Reed.

*   *The said Eliza, John, and Georgiana were now clustered round their mama in the drawing-room: she lay reclined on a sofa by the fireside, and with her darlings about her (for the time neither quarrelling nor crying) looked perfectly happy. Me, she had dispensed[1] from joining the group.*

dispensed[1] – banned

❸ Write a comment explaining how this extract moves on from and develops the opening, both in the information it provides and in the further questions it raises. Consider how the writer:

*   Reveals more of the narrator's character and probable age
*   Goes on to hint at the narrator's position within the family
*   Begins to make us sympathise with the narrator

Remember:

*   Stick to the focus of the question – development of ideas.
*   Show how the passage progresses.

STRUCTURING A FICTION TEXT

A passage may be structured in many ways. For example:

- In the **order in which an observer takes in the scene**
- From an **overall picture to fine detail,** or the opposite
- In the **order in which action occurs**, building up to a **climax**
- **Switching time frame,** using memories, action, plans and **foreshadowing**

Read this passage about a young woman moving home. Some of its features have been highlighted.

New paragraph shifts reader's attention to wagon's contents, first objects (furniture), then plants, then living things	**Opening sentence emphasises the young woman being left alone**

The sensible horses stood – perfectly still, and the waggoner's steps sank fainter and fainter in the distance.

The girl on the summit of the load sat motionless, surrounded by tables and chairs with their legs upwards, backed by an oak settle, and ornamented in front by pots of geraniums, myrtles, and cactuses, together with a caged canary – all probably from the windows of the house just vacated. There was also a cat in a willow basket, from the partly opened lid of which she gazed with half-closed eyes, and affectionately surveyed the small birds around.

Switches focus to the girl

Creates atmosphere, referring back to the previous paragraph

The handsome girl waited for some time idly in her place, and the only sound heard in the stillness was the hopping of the canary up and down the perches of its prison. Then she looked attentively downwards. It was not at the bird, nor at the cat; it was at an oblong package tied in paper, and lying between them. She turned her head to learn if the waggoner were coming. He was not yet in sight; and her eyes crept back to the package, her thoughts seeming to run upon what was inside it. At length she drew the article into her lap, and untied the paper covering; a small swing looking-glass was disclosed, in which she proceeded to survey herself attentively. She parted her lips and smiled.

Closer focus on what the girl does, arousing our curiosity

From *Far From the Madding Crowd* by Thomas Hardy

---

❹ Write down a short heading to summarise each paragraph.

❺ Comment on how the final paragraph of this passage is structured. For example, is anything hinted at? How is information revealed?

CONTRAST, CONFLICT AND RESOLUTION

Many stories involve contrast and conflict, usually leading to a **resolution** (the end of conflict), or a climax (the high point of excitement).

In the following extract, the character Cathy reports disagreeing with Linton. As you read, think about how the passage is structured.

> TOP TIP
>
> Look for how information is withheld as well as how it is revealed.

> *'He said the pleasantest manner of spending a hot July day was lying from morning till evening on a bank of heath in the middle of the moors, with the bees humming dreamily about among the bloom, and the larks singing high up overhead, and the blue sky and bright sun shining steadily and cloudlessly. That was his most perfect idea of heaven's happiness: mine was rocking in a rustling green tree, with a west wind blowing, and bright white clouds flitting rapidly above; and not only larks, but throstles[1], and blackbirds, and linnets, and cuckoos pouring out music on every side, and the moors seen at a distance, broken into cool dusky dells; but close by great swells of long grass undulating in waves to the breeze; and woods and sounding water, and the whole world awake and wild with joy. He wanted all to lie in an ecstasy of peace; I wanted all to sparkle and dance in a glorious jubilee. I said his heaven would be only half alive; and he said mine would be drunk: I said I should fall asleep in his; and he said he could not breathe in mine, and began to grow very snappish. At last, we agreed to try both, as soon as the right weather came.'*
>
> From *Wuthering Heights* by Emily Brontë

throstles[1] – thrushes

> TOP TIP
>
> Choose verbs and verb phrases to help you analyse structure, such as 'focuses', 'narrows down', 'balances' and 'brings together'.

EXAM FOCUS

Read this opening to an analysis of contrast and conflict in the passage. Some of its features have been highlighted:

Cathy makes Linton's perfect day sound pleasant but unexciting, and then describes her own, which by contrast is full of movement, colour, sound and life. From 'He wanted ...' the conflict intensifies.

Identifies turning point

Summarises the contrast

Describes the change

APPLYING YOUR SKILLS

❻ Continue the analysis of the passage, making at least two more points.

Remember:

- Consider how the pace is increased.
- Show how the passage develops and reaches a resolution.

PROGRESS LOG [tick the correct box]   Needs more work ☐   Getting there ☐   Under control ☐

FORMING AN INTERPRETATION: EVALUATING A TEXT

HOW DO YOU INTERPRET AND EVALUATE A TEXT?

A04

PAPER 1,
SECTION A, Q4

Question 4 asks you to **evaluate** part of a text **critically** and **support** this with **textual references**. You will have to give a personal response to an aspect of the text, such as **characterisation, setting** and atmosphere, or **themes**. To do so, you will need to consider language effects and comment on how successful you think they are.

Read the extract below. How far does the writer succeed in revealing the narrator's character?

> *It was a great comfort to turn from that chap to my influential friend, the battered, twisted, ruined, tin-pot steamboat. I clambered on board. She rang under my feet like an empty Huntley & Palmer biscuit-tin kicked along a gutter; she was nothing so solid in make, and rather less pretty in shape, but I had expended enough hard work on her to make me love her. No influential friend would have served me better. She had given me a chance to come out a bit – to find out what I could do. No, I don't like work. I had rather laze about and think of all the fine things that can be done. I don't like work – no man does – but I like what is in the work – the chance to find yourself.*
>
> From *Heart of Darkness* by Joseph Conrad

How would you answer this question?

- Think about **your own response** to the character and the reasons for it.
- Focus on the **details** described, the narrator's **language**, and what both **say** about him.
- Choose **examples** of details and language that you find **effective**.
- Comment on how these express the narrator's **character**.

EXAM FOCUS

Read this extract from a successful response. Some of its features have been highlighted:

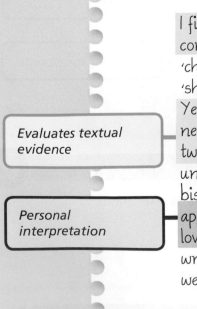

I find the narrator interesting in his contradictions. He prefers his boat to the 'chap' he mentions, affectionately calling it 'she' and 'her', and 'my influential friend'. Yet he disparages the boat with a string of negative physical adjectives – 'battered, twisted, ruined, tin-pot', and compares it unfavourably and unflatteringly with a biscuit tin in the gutter. However, this apparently dim view seems to disguise his love for the boat. I think that the way the writer presents the man is effective because we get a sense of his complicated character: ...

Topic sentence summarises personal response

Evaluates textual evidence

Personal interpretation

❶ Reread the extract, then add a point interpreting and evaluating what the narrator says about his attitude towards work.

NOW YOU TRY IT

Read this further passage from *Heart of Darkness*, then answer the question below.

Going up that river was like travelling back to the earliest beginnings of the world, when vegetation rioted on the earth and the big trees were kings. An empty stream, a great silence, an impenetrable forest. The air was warm, thick, heavy, sluggish. There was no joy in the brilliance of sunshine. The long stretches of the waterway ran on, deserted, into the gloom of overshadowed distances. On silvery sand-banks hippos and alligators sunned themselves side by side. The broadening waters flowed through a mob of wooded islands; you lost your way on that river as you would in a desert, and butted all day long against shoals[1], trying to find the channel, till you thought yourself bewitched.

shoals[1] – shallows

❷ A reader has commented that the way this passage is written makes the jungle voyage convincingly real. How far do you agree?

Remember:

- Give your own impressions.
- Evaluate how the writer has created them.
- Support your views with textual evidence.

THE LANGUAGE OF EVALUATION

It can be particularly useful to have some **adjectives** (or phrases meaning similar things) at your fingertips to explain whether a text is effective or not. For example, consider using words such as:

- 'intense', 'memorable', or 'powerful' (leaves a lasting impression)
- 'vivid' or 'colourful' (strong, bright or rich imagery)
- 'engaging', 'compelling' or 'enticing' (drawing you in)
- 'dramatic' (full of tension and action)

Always make sure the comments you select fit with what you have been asked to focus on.

SUPPORT IDEAS USING EVIDENCE FROM THE TEXT

Question 4 in the exam may remind you to support your opinions with references to the text. This means providing evidence. You could use several types of evidence, depending on what aspect of the text you are asked to comment on:

- What characters do and say
- How the writer uses descriptive language
- What details are included
- Ideas that the text raises or explores

❸ Find an example of each type of evidence about the character Errol in the passage below. Then decide which you would need to support with a quotation and which you could simply refer to.

> *Errol looked at his watch again and drummed his fingers on the desk. 'Come on, come on!' he said aloud, his haunted face creasing tightly. He felt trapped, vulnerable, like a mouse with no hole to run to. Even the stuffed owl in the shadowy corner of the ill-lit basement room seemed to be glaring at him as if he were prey.*

TOP TIP

The source text(s) will be chosen for their literary merit, so focus on what you find effective. Avoid suggesting improvements.

PEE AND PEA

You may have been taught the PEE or PEA techniques:

- PEE – Point, Evidence, Explanation
- PEA – Point, Evidence, Analysis

PEA is more useful, as **analysis** is a higher-level skill than **explanation**. However, for Question 4 you also need **evaluation**, showing your assessment of the writer's skills.

If you use PEA, try not to list the PEA and Evaluation in the same order every time. You do not need to evaluate in every point you make.

Read this paragraph.

GET IT RIGHT!

To achieve a high mark you must **evaluate** the text if the task requires it. This means assessing how far it has achieved its purpose – normally to bring to life the characters or events being described.

Point   Evidence

Errol is portrayed as anxious, in that he looks repeatedly at his watch and drums on the table. These actions are an effective way to show that he is tensely waiting for something to happen.

Analysis and evaluation

Now look at this new version of the paragraph.

> *Errol's repeated glances at his watch and his drumming on the table are effective ways to show that he is tensely waiting for something, revealing his anxious nature.*

❹ Identify the PEA and Evaluation in the second version.

❺ Rewrite the following sentences to vary the PEA and Evaluation order. Start: 'A persuasive sense of menace is created by ...'

> *The character feels in danger, as shown by the adjectives 'trapped, vulnerable', and the strong verb 'glaring', implying threat. The word choices create a persuasive sense of menace.*

EXAM FOCUS

Read this response to Question 2 on page 37, about the first person narrative in the extract from *Heart of Darkness*.

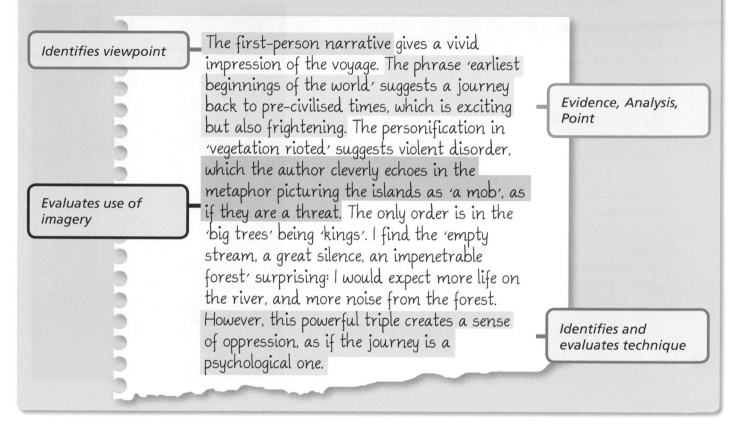

Identifies viewpoint

The first-person narrative gives a vivid impression of the voyage. The phrase 'earliest beginnings of the world' suggests a journey back to pre-civilised times, which is exciting but also frightening. The personification in 'vegetation rioted' suggests violent disorder, which the author cleverly echoes in the metaphor picturing the islands as 'a mob', as if they are a threat. The only order is in the 'big trees' being 'kings'. I find the 'empty stream, a great silence, an impenetrable forest' surprising: I would expect more life on the river, and more noise from the forest. However, this powerful triple creates a sense of oppression, as if the journey is a psychological one.

Evidence, Analysis, Point

Evaluates use of imagery

Identifies and evaluates technique

What mistakes **might** a student have made in answering this question?

- They might have summarised the story of the passage.
- They might have just given a personal response (*'It's like when we went to Center Parcs ...'*).
- They might have missed the connections between parts of the text.
- They might have failed to provide textual evidence.

Read this further extract from *Heart of Darkness*:

> *Trees, trees, millions of trees, massive, immense, running up high; and at their foot, hugging the bank against the stream, crept the little begrimed steamboat, like a sluggish beetle crawling on the floor of a lofty portico.[1] It made you feel very small, very lost, and yet it was not altogether depressing, that feeling. After all, if you were small, the grimy beetle crawled on – which was just what you wanted it to do.*
>
> *portico[1] – roof supported by columns in classical architecture*

6 How far do you agree that the author effectively portrays the narrator's experience?

APPLYING YOUR SKILLS

Read this extract from Susan Hill's novel *The Woman in Black*, then answer the question below.

Baffled, I stood and waited, straining to listen through the mist. What I heard next chilled and horrified me, even though I could neither understand nor account for it. The noise of the pony trap grew fainter and then stopped abruptly and away on the marsh was a curious draining, sucking, churning sound, which went on, together with the shrill neighing and whinnying of a horse in panic, and then I heard another cry, a shout, a terrified sobbing – it was hard to decipher – but with horror I realized that it came from a child, a young child. I stood absolutely helpless in the mist that clouded me and everything from my sight, almost weeping in an agony of fear and frustration, and I knew that I was hearing, beyond any doubt, appalling last noises of a pony and trap, carrying a child in it.

From *The Woman in Black* by Susan Hill

❼ What are your impressions of the **mood** of this extract? Evaluate how the author creates this mood.

Remember:

- Give your impressions.
- Analyse how they are formed.
- Evaluate the text.
- Include evidence in the form of paraphrase or quotations.

PROGRESS CHECK FOR CHAPTER 2

GOOD PROGRESS

I can:

- Identify explicit and implicit information ☐
- Clearly explain most effects of the writer's language choices ☐
- Select a range of suitable quotations to support my ideas ☐

EXCELLENT PROGRESS

I can:

- Analyse thoughtfully the effects of the writer's language choices ☐
- Select the most appropriate quotations to support my ideas ☐
- Interpret and evaluate a text ☐

CHAPTER 3: Paper 1, Section B: Writing descriptive and narrative texts

WHAT'S IT ALL ABOUT?

In Paper 1, Section B of your English Language exam, you will respond to a stimulus such as a title or a photograph by writing a story, part of a story or an imaginative description.

TIMING AND APPROACH

You should spend about forty-five minutes on this section, including planning. Whatever the task set, you will need these core skills:

- Adopt an appropriate writing style (for example, using vivid description).
- Choose interesting ideas that are raised by the question.
- Organise your writing for clarity and interest, using paragraphs with **connectives** and **discourse markers** to link them where necessary.
- Create striking effects in your writing – for example, creating a sense of place and character by using **imagery** such as **similes** and **metaphors**.
- Use accurate grammar, spelling and punctuation.

> **TOP TIP** ★
>
> In the months leading up to the exam, focus on developing key skills that you can then use on the day. For example, to extend your vocabulary read as much fiction as you can and note any new words that appeal to you.

EARNING THE MARKS

There are 80 marks for the whole of Paper 1, and 40 marks are for section B. These are broken down as follows:

- 24 marks for content and organisation – ideas, style and structure
- 16 marks for technical accuracy – spelling, punctuation and grammar

REGISTER AND VOICE

You should write in **Standard English** unless you are writing dialogue, when more informal language might be appropriate. Occasionally, a first-person narrator might use non-standard forms too. Think about the voice of the story. How will it sound? Will you use **dialect** and **colloquialisms**?

EFFECTIVE DESCRIPTIVE WRITING

WHAT MAKES A DESCRIPTION LEAVE A STRONG IMPRESSION ON THE READER?

PAPER 1, SECTION B

There is a difference between description in a purely descriptive piece of writing and description in a story when you are writing in the exam:

- When writing a story, you need to move the plot along and cannot spend too much time on description.
- In a purely descriptive piece, you have more time to consider the detail and **imagery** you want to use.

SHOW DON'T TELL

When you 'tell' a reader something, you are simply informing them. 'Showing' is a technique that helps a reader to visualise what you are describing, making your writing more vivid and exciting.

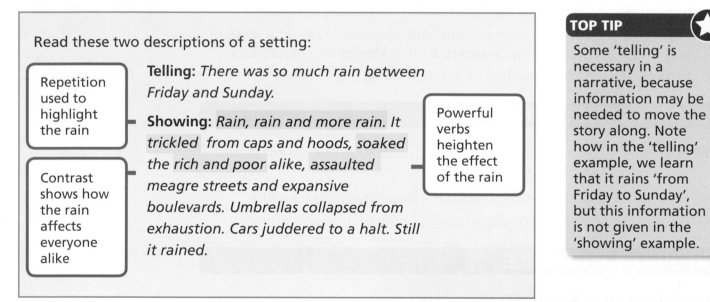

Read these two descriptions of a setting:

> **Repetition used to highlight the rain**

> **Contrast shows how the rain affects everyone alike**

Telling: *There was so much rain between Friday and Sunday.*

Showing: *Rain, rain and more rain. It trickled from caps and hoods, soaked the rich and poor alike, assaulted meagre streets and expansive boulevards. Umbrellas collapsed from exhaustion. Cars juddered to a halt. Still it rained.*

> **Powerful verbs heighten the effect of the rain**

TOP TIP ⭐

Some 'telling' is necessary in a narrative, because information may be needed to move the story along. Note how in the 'telling' example, we learn that it rains 'from Friday to Sunday', but this information is not given in the 'showing' example.

❶ What specific things are **shown** in the second description? (If you were drawing a picture, what would be in it?)

❷ Find an example of **personification** in the second description.

DESCRIBING A PERSON

You can use the same method of 'telling' or 'showing' when describing a person. For example:

Telling: *Nina was completely drenched.*

Showing: *Rivulets of water streamed from Nina's hair and ran down her forehead on to her nose. Water dripped from her coat into her already waterlogged shoes, which squelched with every miserable step she took.*

❸ What specific things does the writer **show** us in this description? Find:

- Powerful verbs
- Vivid **adjectives**
- Repetition
- Other vocabulary choices you think add to the description

If you continued the description about Nina using 'telling', it might read like this:

Useful sentence giving information

Too close to where? Needs to show where Nina is and what the bus looked like

Nina reached the bus stop. As the bus came round the corner, it came too close and she got wet again.

Needs more vivid description showing how she 'got wet'

❹ Rewrite the 'telling' example above using the 'showing' technique to create a vivid picture. You can write more than one sentence. You could begin: 'As the [add adjectives] bus veered round the corner …'

- Use specific, detailed verbs, rather than 'came', 'got wet'.
- Use literary techniques, such as a simile.

TOP TIP

Most images appeal to the sense of sight, but you can also appeal to the other senses (sound, touch, taste). Note how Nina's 'waterlogged' shoes 'squelched'. The image appeals to the senses of sound and touch.

GET IT RIGHT!

Avoid **tautology**. For example, if you use a powerful verb you do not need an adverb with a similar meaning to describe it: 'He **strolled slowly** along the street. To 'stroll' is to walk slowly so you do not need the adverb here.

APPLYING YOUR SKILLS

❺ Write a description of 100 words about a small fishing boat in a storm. Use the picture to help you.

Remember:

- Appeal to the senses.
- 'Show' rather than 'tell', using powerful verbs, adjectives and **adverbs**, comparisons such as **similes** and personification.

CREATING ATMOSPHERE AND MOOD

HOW DO LANGUAGE FEATURES SUCH AS PUNCTUATION OR VARIED SENTENCES CREATE EFFECTS?

AO6

PAPER 1, SECTION B

Punctuation, repetition and a variety of sentence lengths can help to create different **moods**, tension and pace.

Read the extract below:

> *And this Thing I saw? How can I describe it? A monstrous tripod, higher than many houses, striding over the young pine trees, and smashing them aside in its career; a walking engine of glittering metal, striding now across the heather, articulate ropes of steel dangling from it, and the clattering tumult of its passage mingling with the riot of the thunder.*
>
> From *War of the Worlds* by H. G. Wells

❶ Sum up the mood of this extract by choosing the best words from the following:

| surprise | alarm | horror | fear | dismay | excitement |

❷ The table below shows how punctuation and sentence length contribute to the mood of the extract. Find each example in the passage above.

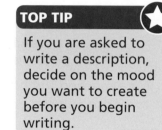

TOP TIP

If you are asked to write a description, decide on the mood you want to create before you begin writing.

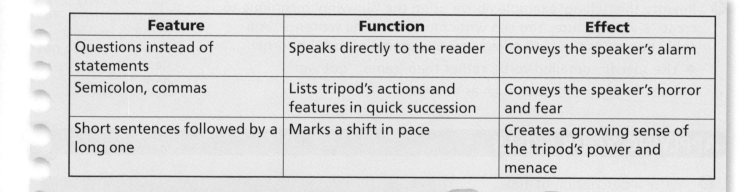

Feature	Function	Effect
Questions instead of statements	Speaks directly to the reader	Conveys the speaker's alarm
Semicolon, commas	Lists tripod's actions and features in quick succession	Conveys the speaker's horror and fear
Short sentences followed by a long one	Marks a shift in pace	Creates a growing sense of the tripod's power and menace

RHETORICAL QUESTIONS

A **rhetorical question** is a question that expects no answer, usually because the answer is obvious or there is no answer. A rhetorical question can be used for effect, to:

● Emphasise a point

● Encourage the reader to accept a particular point of view

● Contemplate the unanswerable

❸ What effect do each of these rhetorical questions have?

- *I'm sure you'd agree with me, wouldn't you?*
- *Who can say what will happen in this world?*
- *Can we get the show on the road, please?*

EXAM FOCUS

Read this successful description of a pleasant surprise. Some of its qualities have been highlighted:

Short sentence followed by a long one changes pace

Mimi gasped. The food was displayed on a crisp white tablecloth: cheeses, pickles, brown rolls, white rolls, pizza, samosas, pakoras, sausage rolls, patties, meringues, eclairs, angel cake, banana cake, chocolate cake and more. Wasn't it just perfect?

Semicolon and commas used to list details

Rhetorical question to emphasise a point

REPETITION

Another way of emphasising a point is by using repetition. Usually the same words and phrases are repeated, but punctuation or sentence length can also be repeated to emphasise mood. For example, asking more than one question (as in the extract from *War of the Worlds*) emphasises the speaker's shock.

Read the following passage:

Quick! Along Mitcham Street I sprint, round the corner and into Pickett's yard. Then up to the far end and into the shadows. I stop. Catch my breath. Steady myself. Lean against the wall. Listen.

Repeating short or minor sentences in succession creates pace and tension and reflects the character's feelings

TOP TIP

Using a series of short sentences to create tension can be effective, but do not overuse this technique otherwise it loses its impact. Use punctuation such as exclamation marks sparingly.

❹ What punctuation is used to create a sense of urgency?

APPLYING YOUR SKILLS

❺ Reread the passage above. Write another paragraph of about 100 words to continue the story. Describe how an unwelcome sound comes closer and closer to the narrator, then slowly fades as the danger passes.

Remember:

- Create tension as the sound comes closer.
- Release the tension as it fades.

PROGRESS LOG [tick the correct box]   Needs more work ▊   Getting there ▊   Under control ▊

GENERATING IDEAS AND STRUCTURING A DESCRIPTION

HOW CAN YOU USE THE STIMULUS GIVEN TO YOU IN THE EXAM EFFECTIVELY?

PAPER 1,
SECTION B

The exam paper will give you a prompt, or stimulus, to inspire your writing. This might be a photograph, a written scenario or a key sentence from a story. There are several ways of using this stimulus to develop your ideas.

WORD CHAINS

You could choose a key word or a feature of the picture to begin. For example, if you are presented with a photograph of the natural world, you might begin your planning by listing the features in the photo to create word chains. A word chain can help you expand your ideas, so it may spark an idea for a description.

First select one feature, such as 'wood'. Write down the next word that comes into your head (such as 'animal'), then continue to do this to create word associations. For example:

> *wood animal rabbit hare field pasture lush summer sun moon stars cosmos mystery*

❶ Create word chains of at least five words starting with each of the following:

mask		fish		lightning		train		despair

FIRST LINES

Another way to generate ideas is to focus on a key word from the stimulus and use it to create an opening sentence. For example, you could generate a sentence around the word 'mask':

> *The mask hung on a nail at the back of the junk shop.*

You can then add detail:

Phrase adds detail   *Adjective adds detail*

> *The mask with the hollow eyes hung from a rusty nail at the back of the junk shop.*

❷ Create first sentences from any of the remaining words in Question 1 (not 'mask').

❸ Copy and complete the sentences below, adding detail with words, phrases and **imagery**. Try to capture such feelings as amazement, delight, sadness, shock or anger.
- *The ... fairground lights, which ... twinkled ... in the dark.*
- *They walked ... along the ... beach for the last time.*
- *The ... laptop, ..., had been completely dismantled.*

STRUCTURE YOUR DESCRIPTION

In the exam, you will need to organise your ideas quickly. Keep them in your head or note them down if you have time. If you were describing the junk shop, you might structure your description in the following way:

- **Paragraph 1:** Begin with a general description of the shop and its atmosphere. Is it mysterious? Enticing? Disturbing?
- **Paragraph 2:** Describe the specific details of the mask and why you were drawn to it.
- **Paragraph 3:** Move on to a different object or introduce a person, etc.

Zoom in on details, using powerful verbs, **adjectives** and **similes**.

Use **prepositions** or **prepositional phrases** to describe the precise relationship of one thing or person to another: 'The key was **inside** a tatty envelope, which had been pushed **behind** the mirror **on** the wall.'

TOP TIP

Remember, moving from a general description (the overall view) to a specific one (a focus on one thing) is a useful technique to use in your writing.

EXAM FOCUS

Read this successful description of a cat. Some of its features have been highlighted:

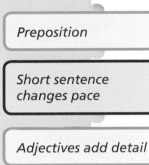

Preposition

Short sentence changes pace

Adjectives add detail

Its tawny eyes were wide open and its long, mottled fur spilled over the pavement like an expensive rug. What a handsome creature it was. It fixed its gaze on me. Should I ask permission to pass? Without warning, it yawned a great, satisfying, pink yawn, lay flat on its luxurious back with its paws in the air and purred.

Simile adds detail

Rhetorical question draws in the reader

APPLYING YOUR SKILLS

❹ Choose one of the following tasks and write a plan for your description.
Describe an occasion when you felt carefree

OR

Write a description suggested by this picture:

Remember:

- Generate some ideas, then draw a box for each paragraph and make notes in each one.
- In the first box write notes for a general description; in the second and third write notes for a specific description.

PROGRESS LOG [tick the correct box] Needs more work ■ Getting there ■ Under control ■

CREATING CONVINCING CHARACTERS AND VOICES

HOW CAN YOU MAKE YOUR CHARACTERS CONVINCING AND VIVID?

PAPER 1, SECTION B

To create a convincing character you should:

- Decide what your character wants. What is their goal (for example, to achieve justice)?
- Consider if they are what they seem (perhaps they have a secret)
- Consider if something is troubling them (are they being threatened?)
- Decide what their strengths and weaknesses are (brave but rash?)

FIRST IMPRESSIONS

The reader's first impression of a character is important. The following description gives an insight into a character as well as her appearance:

Clause showing character's actions

Maggie often listened with her broad arms firmly folded, as if guarding against the influence of a speaker's views – a stance that made her resemble the buffers at the end of a railway line.

Figure of speech showing comparison

❶ Make brief notes saying what sort of person Maggie seems to be. Pay particular attention to the highlighted text.

What a character says and how they respond to others reveals a great deal: In the following **dialogue**, Maggie is protesting against a new road.

> *'I'm not budging!' Maggie insisted, looking up squarely into the eyes of the young police officer from her position in front of the digger.*
>
> *He sighed, and glanced anxiously towards the approaching sergeant. 'Look, Miss, I'm sorry, but you'll have to shift eventually. All the others have given up. You're the last man standing, as it were.'*
>
> *'For your information,' Maggie said evenly, 'I'm a woman. And I'm sitting down. What's more, I'm staying sitting down.'*

❷ What does this extract tell us about Maggie as a person? Think about:
- Her goals (what does she want?)
- Things that might be that troubling or difficult for her

❸ Write five sentences about a teenage son or daughter refusing to do what a parent wants.
- In the first sentence, convey the teenager's personality through their physical movements and appearance (for example, hand gestures).
- The remaining sentences should be dialogue, in which the character reveals more of their personality.

You could start: *'He stood in the kitchen ...'*

TOP TIP ⭐

Writing in the second person (using 'you') can be difficult, but it is very effective when done successfully. Be careful of writing completely in the second person, as this can overwhelm the reader by constantly addressing them directly.

POINT OF VIEW AND VOICE

A narrative can be told from different points of view.

Point of view (POV)	Voice	Effect on reader
First person, 'I'	Intimate	Draws in the reader, who experiences only one POV
Second person, 'you' single or plural	Commanding, urgent	Reader feels as though they are almost a character in the story
Third person, 'he'/'she'/'it'	More distant	Reader is able to experience more than one POV

Most narratives are told in the third or first person. Point of view is important because there are things you could not say in all viewpoints:

- **Third person:** *Joe sat with his head in his strong, capable hands. He was exhausted, yet still looked remarkably handsome.*
- **First person:** *I sat with my head in my strong, capable hands. I was exhausted, yet still looked remarkably handsome.*

❹ What different impressions do you get of the character?

> **TOP TIP** ⭐
>
> What one character says about another also reveals something about the first character's personality. Keep this in mind when writing narratives.

EXAM FOCUS ✎

Read this successful opening, written in the second person:

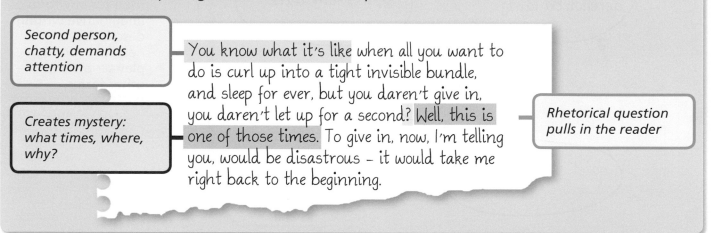

Second person, chatty, demands attention

Creates mystery: what times, where, why?

You know what it's like when all you want to do is curl up into a tight invisible bundle, and sleep for ever, but you daren't give in, you daren't let up for a second? Well, this is one of those times. To give in, now, I'm telling you, would be disastrous – it would take me right back to the beginning.

Rhetorical question pulls in the reader

APPLYING YOUR SKILLS ✔

❺ Write a 100-word character sketch of a market trader who sells fruit and vegetables. Decide what viewpoint to use and add a feature that suggests your character has a secret.

Remember:

- Create a vivid first impression.
- Give your character a goal.

PROGRESS LOG [tick the correct box]   Needs more work ▢   Getting there ▢   Under control ▢

GENERATING IDEAS AND STRUCTURING A NARRATIVE

HOW CAN YOU PLAN A STORY?

A05

In the exam, you may be asked to write a narrative or story. Planning what you are going to write before you start is a key skill.

Look at this question:

Write a story that involves a dangerous situation.

To start planning an answer to this question, you could create a spider diagram with the word 'danger' in the centre. You could then address the following questions:

- Who is in danger?
- What is the danger?
- Where is it happening?

Or you could begin by sketching a quick mental image of your main character, including name, gender, one or two character traits, circumstances (who or what is putting them in danger), appearance. For example:

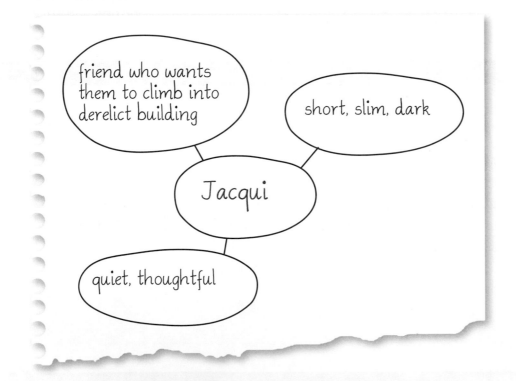

> **TOP TIP**
>
> Creative writing aids, such as word chains and spider diagrams, can be used for any form of imaginative writing: description, narrative, poetry, play scripts and other forms.

❶ Copy the 'character' diagram above and complete it as if you were planning an answer to the question.

❷ Keep the key word 'danger' in mind and think about **who** is in danger – the main character or someone else. Note down some thoughts to start developing your ideas.

CREATE A PLOT

When planning your plot, you need to think about:

- The start of your story (your main character's circumstances)
- Where your story will go (what does the character do, how does this affect the events?)
- How it will end (well or badly?)

Most stories follow a linear structure:

introduction → complication → crisis → climax → resolution

Many narratives have more than one crisis or stage (see Freytag's pyramid on page 96), but you will have limited time in an exam so limit yourself to one key event where everything reaches a **climax**.

The opening should arouse the reader's curiosity, so they want to read on. The conclusion needs to have impact, too. You could end with a twist or a **cliffhanger**:

> *He was caught now, completely and utterly. The prospect that he might stare Death in the face had never once occurred to him.*
> *'Are we ready?' said a voice.*

OTHER NARRATIVE DECISIONS

When planning a narrative, you will also need to consider:

- What **point of view** will you write from – first person ('I') or third person ('he'/'she'/'it') or the unusual second person 'you' (see page 49)
- If you choose the **first person**, will this be the main character or someone else?
- What **tense** will you write in?
- How many other **characters** will you have? (Not too many.) What is their **relationship** to the main character?

❸   Write down answers to these points for the story you are planning.

TOP TIP

Try to include some direct speech, to 'show' rather than 'tell' what the characters are doing and thinking. Make sure it fits naturally with your story.

DIFFERENT NARRATIVE APPROACHES

Some narratives begin at a point in the plot when some or even all of the action has already taken place. This is referred to as *in media res* (Latin for 'in the middle of things'). For example:

> *I peered through a small gap in the fence. I couldn't believe it! There was nothing but rubble with grass growing between the debris. I'd only been away three weeks. Where was the school?*

The events that lead to this moment are revealed throughout the story in various ways, such as description, **dialogue** or **flashback**.

FLASHBACKS

A flashback is an event that has happened at an earlier time and is recalled in the main story as it is being told. It is used to give:

● Essential information that has a bearing on the plot

● Insights into a character's nature and actions

When using flashbacks, make sure you signal them clearly and make it obvious when you return to the main story, otherwise the reader will be confused.

GET IT RIGHT!

Remember, flashbacks can make the story richer, but they take the reader away from the main action, so only use them if they are essential to the story.

EXAM FOCUS

Read this well-constructed use of flashback. Some of its features have been highlighted:

> The moment she saw the street, the old images rose up again: the sunless day, the bare trees, the woman walking towards her, head down, her shoes click-clicking on the pavement. Lina clenched her fists tight, so that her nails sunk into her flesh, but it helped the images fall away. Then she relaxed and continued down the street.

The flashback

Immediately returns to the main story

Clearly signals that a flashback will begin

APPLYING YOUR SKILLS

❹ Add a fifty-word flashback to the extract below. The narrative relates to the theme of danger.

David hauled the faded, velvet armchair through the rickety gate and swung the gate shut with his right boot. It shuddered on its hinges. He grinned.

Remember:

● Signal when the flashback begins and when you return to the main story.

PROGRESS CHECK FOR CHAPTER 3

GOOD PROGRESS

I can:

● Create mood in descriptions, using language effectively ☐

● Create some convincing characters and narrative voices ☐

● Generate sound ideas, and structure descriptions and narratives clearly ☐

EXCELLENT PROGRESS

I can:

● Create a rich atmosphere in descriptions, using detailed and effective language ☐

● Create a range of convincing characters and narrative voices ☐

● Generate original and engaging ideas, and structure descriptions and narratives in imaginative ways to engage the reader ☐

CHAPTER 4: Paper 2, Section A: Reading non-fiction texts

WHAT'S IT ALL ABOUT?

In Paper 2, Section A of the English Language exam, you will answer four questions based on two non-fiction sources: A and B. Source A will be from the twentieth or twenty-first century. Source B will be from the nineteenth century. Both will express viewpoints in some way and be on related topics. They could be in a range of forms, such as magazine articles, news stories, letters or journals.

TIMING AND APPROACH

Spend about an hour on Section A, including up to fifteen minutes carefully reading the sources. You may find it helpful to read the two passages once, then read the questions, then read the sources again, annotating them to help you answer the questions.

The exam paper will tell you what to focus on for each question. This is likely to be:

- Question 1: part of Source A **or** B
- Question 2: both sources
- Question 3: source A **or** B
- Question 4: both sources

Another possible planning approach is to reread and annotate the sources for each question in turn as you answer them. If you follow this approach, make sure you keep a close eye on the clock!

TOP TIP

There are no marks for spelling, punctuation or grammar in Paper 2, Section A, but if you express yourself clearly and accurately it will be easier for the examiner to understand your answers and credit you for them.

EARNING THE MARKS

There are 80 marks for the whole of Paper 2, and 40 marks are for Section A. The table below shows how these are allocated and gives an overview of what you need to do for each question.

PAPER 2, SECTION A

Question	Marks	What you must do
1	4	Choose true statements from a list of statements, some of which are untrue.
2	8	Summarise differences or similarities between the two sources.
3	12	Write an extended analysis of language and/or structure in one of the two sources.
4	16	Write an extended comparison of how the writers of each source convey their attitudes.

For Question 1, you simply have to mark boxes. For the other questions a key skill is being able to support your claims with evidence and analysis.

SOURCE A: TWENTY-FIRST CENTURY NON-FICTION

From 'Why do we read scary books?'

Lou Morgan, *The Guardian,* **29 October 2015 (theguardian.com)**

Some of my favourite books when I was 13 or so were horror stories. Point Horror, Stephen King, Bram Stoker, James Herbert … all the names you'd expect to see on the list. I used to sneak into second-hand bookshops and buy anthologies of vampire stories, smuggling them home in my bag or my coat because my mother didn't
5 approve. 'They'll scare you,' she always said. And she was right – they did. But that was the point.

Fear is one of our primal emotions: it's one that is hardwired into us, just as it is in all animals. On a very basic level it has kept us alive as a species; encouraging us to stay away from long drops and big fires, helping us dodge sabre-tooth tigers and other
10 Things With Big Sharp Teeth And Claws that might quite enjoy adding us to their dinner. Last time I looked though, there weren't too many sabre-tooth tigers to worry about on my local high street.

We're a peculiar lot, when you think about it: we work so hard to make our world, our environment safer … and then we actively seek out things that will make us afraid.
15 Horror movies, urban legends, ghost stories. We hunt down the darkness and we revel in it. Why? Because, this way, we can control it.

When I asked my corner of Twitter what scared them (in a very quick and – admittedly – deeply unscientific survey), I got answers ranging from "human cruelty" to "being insignificant". Imprisonment – both in a place and in our own bodies. Abandonment.
20 Helplessness. Pain, loss and grief. These are the big things that frighten us, the things we think could destroy us. These are the things that keep us up at night. *These* are the new sabre-tooth tigers.

The difference is that if you're faced with a sabre-tooth tiger, a spear is going to make you feel a lot better about your odds of survival. How do we battle the fear of losing
25 the people we love, and being powerless to stop it? How do we face that down?

Simple. We seek out stories; stories which give us a place to put our fears. Books in particular let us pour our fear into them before we have so much of it sloshing around in our heads that we drown in it. Stories that frighten us or unsettle us – not just horror stories, but ones that make us uncomfortable or that strike a chord somewhere
30 deep inside – give us the means to explore the things that scare us … but only as far as our imaginations and our experiences allow. They keep us safe while letting us imagine we're in peril. Stories, after all, are never *about* what they're about: there is always a pocket somewhere within them for us to drop in our own emotions, our own fears. A box right at the heart of it all waiting to be filled, somewhere we can lift up
35 the lid and look at the darkness … and close it again when we've had enough.

There is always space for us at the middle of a story – any story. We make it ours just by reading it. A book is a perfectly personalised map through the nightmare forest, because we already know where the monsters are. We put them there ourselves.

Horror stories reflect their times: just as the repressed Victorians loved their vampires,
40 we seem to gravitate towards technology, zombies, dystopia and psychological terrors. When I wrote my own horror novel, *Sleepless*, I wanted to add the intense pressures and stresses of exams into that mix – and (particularly as someone with a long, slightly embattled history of manic depression) the fear of not being able to trust your own mind.

SOURCE B: NINETEENTH-CENTURY NON-FICTION

Reverend Lord Sidney Goldolphin Osborne, letter to *The Times*, 1864

The author claims that doctors are often called to the bedsides of restless, fearful and sleepless children who, rather than having a physical illness, are really suffering from reading the wrong books: '... reading which, keeping the mind on the strain, has wrought it up to an excitement from which it cannot calm down by any power of its own'. He continues:

It is quite true that there are many most excellent books for the amusement of young children. I have seen some I hold to be most pernicious,[1] which are yet considered quite harmless ... I once took up and read in the nursery of a friend a book which in you or me might only raise a smile, but which I am satisfied might give the children

5 for whom it was written night after night of pure terror. It was written something after this fashion: It was the history of two truant kittens, which in a fit of naughty disobedience had absconded[2] from home. Their adventures were many; they were cleverly told in child language; they were such as must interest a child deeply in the fate of the brother and sister catlings; there were beautifully executed pictures of

10 such things as awful owls with eyes of fire hovering over them at night, murderous-looking dogs coming down on them by day, bulls breathing from their nostrils as if they were chimneys on fire, bandit cats, giants awfully armed, seizing them to carry them to dark caves, etc.

Of course, the moral was, kittens and children who are disobedient will be subject to

15 such terrible tribulations. It struck me that such a book was enough to scare sleep from any young child allowed to pore over its pages; many such tales would make it subject to the dreams and screams which, terrifying the parents, invoke the [doctor]; they then all say it is stomach [ache], and proceed to inflict all kinds of intestinal torture to no purpose, for the child, confined to its bed, is given more and more of

20 such intoxicating literature. Weakened by the senna[3] and traditional grey powder, it gets worse and worse; the [doctor] is puzzled, the mother alarmed; more advice is called in; the child is sent to the sea, there gets well under the more novel and natural fascination of shells and seaweed. Fortunately the books are left behind; it is forbidden to read at all, but not because what it read was bad reading for it.

25 When shall we learn that, just as prudence should dictate the food a child should eat, so should it regulate the food afforded to its brain? There is no greater folly than this system of rubbing off the natural angles of childishness by a course of reading appealing to childish simplicity, but wrapping up amusement in clever mimicry of the most exciting of all literature, the novel. Childish sentiment runs to dumb animals and

30 their young; tales may be written on these to afford the utmost amount of childlike, gleeful interest – may be made joyous as well as instructive. I never fear sleeplessness from over laughing. Children are born to laugh a good deal; it is time enough to excite their tears by sentiment when that season has come when sorrow must mix more or less with their joy.

Glossary:
pernicious[1] – damaging
absconded[2] – run away
senna[3] – a herbal laxative

IDENTIFYING CORRECT INFORMATION

HOW SHOULD YOU DEAL WITH THE QUESTION?

PAPER 2,
SECTION A, Q1

This is likely to be a relatively straightforward multiple-choice question designed to ease you into the exam. There are only 4 marks, so spend about five minutes on it. If this is the case, you should shade four boxes to indicate true statements.

The statements will not directly quote the passage, so you will have to interpret them, relating their wording to the information in the passage. For example, reread this sentence from Source A:

> *Point Horror, Stephen King, Bram Stoker, James Herbert ... all the names you'd expect to see on the list.*

This tells us that the writer read horror stories by a number of authors, as well as from the Point Horror series. You may have heard of one or two of them. The phrase 'all the names you'd expect to see on the list' tells us that she read popular horror authors.

❶ Would the following statement be correct? Explain your answer.

Lou Morgan read horror stories by little-known authors.

The second half of Morgan's sentence should make the answer clear.

❷ Consider these statements, which relate to paragraphs 1–3 of Source A.

A Vampire stories have never frightened Lou Morgan.

B Morgan thinks fear can be useful.

C Morgan thinks that human beings are contradictory.

D Morgan's mother disapproved of her reading fiction.

E According to Morgan, humans want to control what they fear.

F Morgan used to steal books and smuggle them into her house.

G As a teenager, Morgan read books by a variety of authors.

H Morgan thinks the modern world is just as dangerous as the Stone Age world.

Decide which four statements are correct. Write down the letters.

EXAM FOCUS

Read the comments below to see how you might be confused by the statements.

A You might think this is true because Morgan says that some of her 'favourite' books were horror stories.

B You might think this is false because Morgan says that many dangers faced by ancient peoples no longer exist.

C This requires you to interpret the phrase *'We're a peculiar lot'*.

D This could mislead you by presenting a statement that is only partly true: her mother only disapproved of her reading horror fiction.

E This requires you to understand that 'what they fear' in the statement refers to 'the darkness' in the passage.

F This is another partially true statement. A careless reading could make you think that it is true. Morgan used to smuggle books into her house, but she did not steal them.

G Several authors are mentioned: a variety of authors.

H She does not say that there are no dangers in the modern world; nor does she say that life is as dangerous as ever. When she mentions *'sabre-tooth tigers and other Things With Big Sharp Teeth And Claws'*, she implies that life now is less dangerous than it once was.

APPLYING YOUR SKILLS

❸ Decide which four statements below are correct. They relate to paragraphs 4–6 of Source A.

A Lou Morgan carried out thorough research into the causes of human fear.

B According to Morgan, people have a wide range of fears.

C Morgan says people feel better about threats if they feel equipped to tackle them.

D Morgan says we all have a fear of drowning.

E Morgan says that only horror stories can help us to cope with fear.

F Morgan says that imagination is important in coping with fear.

G According to Morgan, stories mean exactly what they appear to mean.

H Morgan points out that we can choose when to stop reading a story.

Remember:

● Read the statements carefully.

● Look for information relating to them in the section of the text indicated in the question.

● Identify the part of the section the statement seems to relate to by locating key words.

SUMMARISING AND SYNTHESISING FROM TWO TEXTS

HOW CAN YOU COMPARE TWO TEXTS?

A01

PAPER 2,
SECTION A, Q2

Question 2 is meant to prepare you for comparing the two texts in detail in Question 4. For Question 2, you will just need to **summarise differences**. A typical question, based on our Sources A and B, might be:

*Use details from **both** sources. Write a summary of the differences in their attitudes to young people's reading.*

APPROACHES

Begin by underlining or highlighting relevant phrases and sentences in both sources. Then, make a quick list for each source. When you write the answer, you have two options:

- Deal with **one source, then the other**, linking your comments with a phrase such as 'Osborne, on the other hand ...'.

- **Intertwine** your comments on each source.

The first approach is more straightforward, but the second will encourage you to compare different aspects of the attitudes of the two writers.

SUMMARISING

To summarise, identify the most important ideas then put them in your own words, using fewer words and less detail. For example, you might replace 'apples, pears and bananas' with 'fruit'.

Reread Source A. Its second paragraph could be summarised like this:

- *Being scared by horror stories and similar fiction can be beneficial.*

- *Fear has helped the human race to survive.*

❶ Here is a summary of some more attitudes in Source A that broadly relate to 'young people's reading'. Find evidence for each in the source.

- *Humans used to be afraid of physical threats, but now they are more likely to fear abstract or irrational things, such as 'being insignificant'.*

- *Humans need to feel in control of what they fear.*

- *Horror stories reflect the times in which they are written.*

❷ Make a similar list of attitudes in Source B. As in the list above, summarise the attitudes, using your own words where possible.

> **TOP TIP** ⭐
>
> Using your own words will encourage you to be brief and show that you understand the source. If it is not obvious where your information comes from, give a short quotation with an explanation.

USING LANGUAGE TO COMPARE

The student summary above **compares** different aspects of each text in turn. If you follow this approach, you will need to use **link words** and phrases effectively.

The following table shows some useful link words and phrases. All of them could be used at the start or in the middle of a sentence.

Word/phrase	Example	Function
On the other hand	*Osborne, on the other hand, ...*	Present a difference or contradiction
Whereas	*Morgan sees fear as positive, whereas Osborne thinks ...*	Present a difference
Unlike	*Unlike Morgan, Osborne sees nothing positive in fear ...*	Present a difference
In contrast with	*Osborne, in contrast with Morgan, is concerned about ...*	Present a difference
Moreover	*He thinks fear is unsettling. Moreover, he claims that it ...*	Present a further point, adding to an argument

EXAM FOCUS

Read a student's summary of the differences in attitude in Sources A and B:

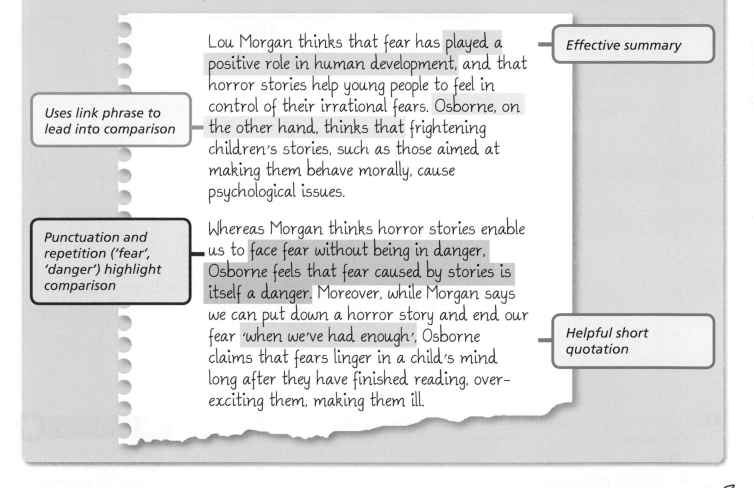

Lou Morgan thinks that fear has played a positive role in human development, and that horror stories help young people to feel in control of their irrational fears. Osborne, on the other hand, thinks that frightening children's stories, such as those aimed at making them behave morally, cause psychological issues.

Whereas Morgan thinks horror stories enable us to face fear without being in danger, Osborne feels that fear caused by stories is itself a danger. Moreover, while Morgan says we can put down a horror story and end our fear 'when we've had enough', Osborne claims that fears linger in a child's mind long after they have finished reading, over-exciting them, making them ill.

Effective summary

Uses link phrase to lead into comparison

Punctuation and repetition ('fear', 'danger') highlight comparison

Helpful short quotation

APPLYING YOUR SKILLS

❸ Read the two sources again, then write your own summary of the **differences in attitude** towards children's reading.

PROGRESS LOG [tick the correct box]   Needs more work ▪   Getting there ▪   Under control ▪

UNDERSTANDING PERSUASIVE LANGUAGE

HOW SHOULD YOU ANALYSE PERSUASIVE LANGUAGE IN A TEXT?

A02

PAPER 2,
SECTION A, Q3

Question 3 is based on **one** of the two sources. It could be either one. A typical question for Source B might be:

> *How does Osborne use language to convey his viewpoint?*

How would you answer this question?

- Consider the **register** and **tone** of the text, and how they persuade.
- Underline **phrases** and **sentences** that you find persuasive.
- Make notes analysing the **effect** of these phrases and sentences.
- Select phrases and describe their effects.

The table below outlines some of these effects.

TOP TIP ⭐

The non-fiction sources you are given will not always be explicitly persuasive, but they will usually express a particular perspective or take on things.

Phrase	Effect
'most pernicious ... quite harmless'	The writer contrasts the negative adjective 'pernicious' with the simple 'quite harmless', suggesting how wrong the latter view is.
'night after night of pure terror'	The writer repeats 'night' and uses the adjective–noun combination 'pure terror' to stress the children's intense and sustained suffering.
'adventures', 'cleverly told in child language' 'interest a child deeply', 'beautifully executed pictures'	The writer uses positive phrases to emphasise the stories' appeal to children, before describing their harmful effects. The contrast emphasises his point
'awful owls with eyes of fire'	One of several vivid visual details used by the writer, helping readers to imagine the effect on children.
'terrible tribulations'	The writer's use of 'tribulations' – a powerful formal word for ordeals or hardships – makes the judgement on children seem very harsh, especially when emphasised by **alliteration**.

❶ Following the examples in the table, analyse the persuasive effect of the following phrases. Try to say which technique is being used in each case.

- *'dreams and screams'*
- *'all kinds of intestinal torture'*
- *'intoxicating literature'*

TOP TIP ⭐

Not all source texts will be explicitly persuasive, but they will have a particular perspective on an event or topic.

ANALYSING DEVICES AND SENTENCE STRUCTURES

In addition to commenting on the effect of words and phrases, you should also comment on persuasive language devices such as:

- **Rhetorical questions** (e.g. *'Have we all gone mad?'*)
- **Triads** (lists of three)
- **Alliteration** (as in *'terrible tribulations'*)
- **Imagery** (**metaphors, similes, personification**)

In addition, comment on sentence structures. For example, sentences may have an overall rhetorical effect, such as Osborne's long sentence beginning, *'Their adventures were many ...'*. This lists ways in which the book would appeal to children, with the list items gradually lengthening to build to a climax of frightening pictures.

TOP TIP

A good way to understand the effect of a word choice is to ask yourself how the effect would be different if a different word with a similar meaning had been used.

EXAM FOCUS

Read this successful analysis of the effects of Source B. Some of its qualities have been highlighted:

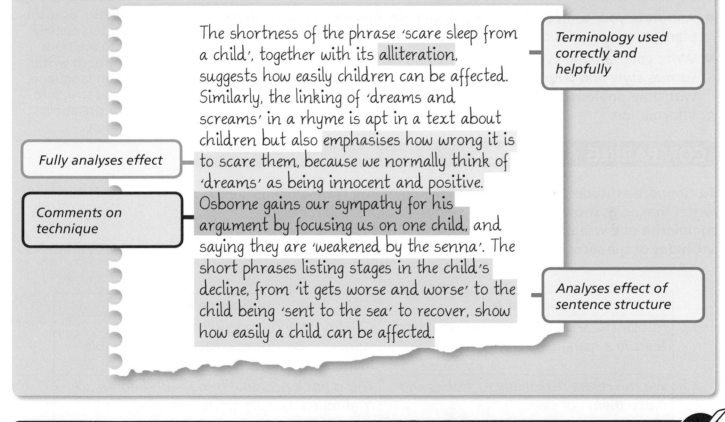

The shortness of the phrase 'scare sleep from a child', together with its alliteration, suggests how easily children can be affected. Similarly, the linking of 'dreams and screams' in a rhyme is apt in a text about children but also emphasises how wrong it is to scare them, because we normally think of 'dreams' as being innocent and positive. Osborne gains our sympathy for his argument by focusing us on one child, and saying they are 'weakened by the senna'. The short phrases listing stages in the child's decline, from 'it gets worse and worse' to the child being 'sent to the sea' to recover, show how easily a child can be affected.

Terminology used correctly and helpfully

Fully analyses effect

Comments on technique

Analyses effect of sentence structure

APPLYING YOUR SKILLS

❷ Write an analysis of how the final paragraph of Source B uses persuasive language.

Remember:

- Select persuasive words and phrases and analyse their effect.
- Use the correct terms for language devices if you know them, and analyse their effect.
- Comment on the effects of sentence structures.

PROGRESS LOG [tick the correct box]   Needs more work ☐   Getting there ☐   Under control ☐

COMPARING WRITERS' VIEWPOINTS AND TECHNIQUES

HOW CAN YOU COMPARE ATTITUDES AND TECHNIQUES IN TWO TEXTS?

PAPER 2, SECTION A, Q4

A typical Question 4 based on the sources in this chapter might be:

Compare how the two writers convey their different attitudes to stories.

In your answer, you should:

- Compare their different **attitudes**
- Compare the **methods** they use to convey their attitudes
- Support your ideas with **quotations** from both texts

How would you answer this question?

- Decide what the writers' **different attitudes** are – your answer to Question 2 will help with this.

- Select **quotations as evidence** for these attitudes.

- **Annotate** your sources and, if you have time, make two quick lists to **plan** your comments on their **methods**.

- Write your answer, in paragraphs, moving from **attitudes** to **methods**, such as **style and structure**. Your answer to Question 3 should help with your analysis of one of the texts, but do not simply repeat information.

> **GET IT RIGHT!** ⭐
>
> The phrase 'how the two writers convey' refers to methods used by each writer, including language, form and structure. Try to write about **all** of these.

COMPARING ATTITUDES

To compare attitudes, you need to briefly summarise the main points each writer makes, as shown in the table below. You may find it helpful to summarise one writer, for example starting with Source A, then add the attitudes of the second that are either similar or very different.

Source A	Source B
Horror stories help us to confront our fears in a manageable way.	*Children cannot cope with frightening stories: these stories create unmanageable fears.*
We can relate personally to stories and make them our own.	*This is not a personal thing – all children are frightened by scary stories and may get ill because of them.*

IDENTIFYING STYLE AND TECHNIQUES

Read some of the techniques used in Source A paragraphs 1–3.

- Morgan uses an **anecdote** about her teenage book-buying habits.
- She **lists** authors and, later, things we 'seek out' to 'make us afraid'.
- She **quotes** her mother ('They'll scare you'), then **surprises** us by agreeing with her.

- She **uses humour** – using capitals for 'Things With Big Sharp Teeth And Claws', that are made to sound amusingly civilised 'adding us to their dinner'.

- She **entertains** us with the surprising image of sabre-tooth tigers on 'my local high street'.

- She **asks the question** 'Why?', then answers it.

❶ Read the rest of Source A.

- Make a list of language techniques used in the remainder of the source.

- Decide which are the most important, and what short quotations you could use as evidence for them.

- Compare Lou Morgan's techniques with those used by Osborne in Source B. Make notes on their similarities and differences.

EXAM FOCUS

Read this successful extract comparing techniques in the texts:

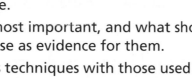

Both authors use anecdote. Morgan describes her own teenage book-buying, which she then justifies ('that was the point'), while Osborne describes a children's book he once picked up. Morgan, however, uses more humour. In 'dodge sabre-tooth tigers', the informal verb has a comic effect, and her description of animals 'that might quite enjoy adding us to their dinner' also uses wittily ironic understatement to joke about our fears.

> *Topic sentence states a basic similarity*

> *Embedded quotation with analysis of effect and purpose of style*

While Osborne uses some humour, as in 'catlings', on the whole he is more serious. His strong, negative adjective 'pernicious' conveys the serious effects on children, and he evokes our sympathy in 'night after night of pure terror', in which repetition emphasises the effect, and 'terrible tribulations', which strongly conveys the children's suffering, emphasised by alliteration.

> *Linking phrase identifies a similarity and prepares for a contrast*

> *Fluently expresses effect*

WRITING ABOUT STRUCTURE

Compare the writers' use of structure as a technique. To do this, try to get an overview of how each source develops. Think of a short heading that would sum up the attitudes or arguments in each paragraph. There are some examples over the page.

TOP TIP ⭐

Although both texts will express a viewpoint, they may have different purposes and target audiences, which will influence their style.

For Source A, these might begin with:

- *Morgan's teenage love of horror stories*
- *The importance of fear*
- *Our attraction to horror*
- *Modern fears*

EXAM FOCUS

Here is how a student might have written about the structure of Morgan's text:

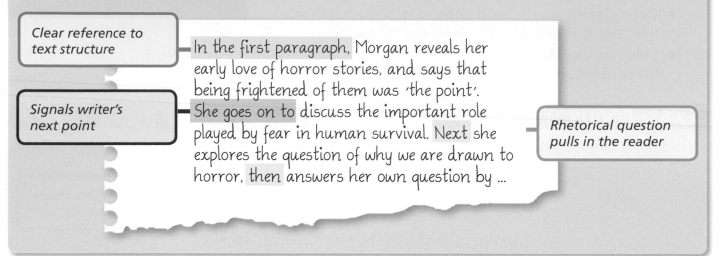

Clear reference to text structure

Signals writer's next point

In the first paragraph, Morgan reveals her early love of horror stories, and says that being frightened of them was 'the point'. She goes on to discuss the important role played by fear in human survival. Next she explores the question of why we are drawn to horror, then answers her own question by ...

Rhetorical question pulls in the reader

❷ Reread Source B. Find similar short headings to sum up the three paragraphs.

APPLYING YOUR SKILLS

❸ Write a response to the question at the start of this unit, which asks you to compare how the two writers convey their different attitudes to stories in the two sources.

Remember:

- Use the bullet points in the question to help you cover all its aspects.
- Write about differences in attitude, then in style and structure.
- Select quotations as evidence and analyse their effects.

PROGRESS CHECK FOR CHAPTER 4

GOOD PROGRESS

I can:

- Identify true statements and summarise attitudes ☐
- Analyse word choices and some techniques ☐

EXCELLENT PROGRESS

I can:

- Compare attitudes ☐
- Compare register and word choices thoroughly and effectively ☐
- Compare techniques and their effects in detail using correct terminology ☐

CHAPTER 5: Paper 2, Section B: Writing to present a viewpoint

WHAT'S IT ALL ABOUT?

In Paper 2, Section B of your English Language exam, you will answer one question, expressing your views on an issue related to the theme of the sources in Section A. You will be told what **form** to write in – for example, a letter, a speech or a magazine article.

TIMING AND APPROACH

If you have spent an hour on Section A, you will then have forty-five minutes for Section B. You should aim to spend about five minutes planning. It is also very important to allow five minutes at the end to check and improve your work.

> **TOP TIP** ⭐
>
> Use the mark allocation table as a checklist for the aspects of written English you think you need to work on.

EARNING THE MARKS

There are 80 marks for the whole of Paper 2, and 40 marks are for Section B. The table below shows how these marks are allocated.

PAPER 2, SECTION B

Marks	What you will be marked on	What this means
24	Content and organisation	Content: ● Your ideas ● How well you have fitted your writing to the given purpose and audience Organisation: ● The fluency of your writing and mastery of language techniques ● Structure and paragraphing
16	Technical accuracy	Sentence structure ● Vocabulary ● Spelling, punctuation and grammar ● Appropriate **register** (degree of formality) and use of **Standard English** (without slang, **dialect** or non-standard grammar)

WHAT IS WRITING TO EXPRESS A VIEWPOINT?

WHAT ARE 'EXPRESSING' AND 'PERSUADING'?

PAPER 2,
SECTION B

When writing to **express** a viewpoint, you are aiming to **persuade** readers to agree with you. However, your expectations will depend on the **purpose** of the writing. For example:

- In a magazine article about reality TV, you may just want readers to sympathise with your views and be entertained by them.

- In a job application or a letter to voters, you will want to do everything you can to persuade your readers and make them act in a particular way, because you will benefit if they do so.

These differences show the importance of three factors:

- **Purpose:** what the writing is intended to do (for example, persuade readers to vote for you)

- **Audience:** who it is aimed at (for example, the age group, level of education, interests, etc.)

- **Form:** where the writing will appear (for example, in a letter, an article, the text for a speech)

In the exam, you may be given a provocative statement, such as:

> *School uniform is an attempt to prevent teenagers from expressing themselves. Few adults are obliged to wear a uniform, so teenagers should not have to either.*

This will be followed by a task that identifies purpose, audience and form, such as:

Form   Audience

Write a letter to your school governors in which you explain your views on this statement.

                  Purpose

❶ Identify the purpose, audience and form in the following exam-style tasks:

- *'Zoos are just animal prisons, out-dated institutions with no place in the modern world.' Write an article for the weekend magazine of a **broadsheet** newspaper explaining your views on this subject.*

- *'Television is the worst thing that ever happened to modern society.' Write the text of a speech intended to influence a group advising the government on its media policies.*

REGISTER AND TONE

Register refers to the type of language used in a text, especially how formal it is. Compare these two comments:

- *Me and my workmates reckon it's time you realised you've got to look after us if we're going to pull out the stops and crack your deadlines. Sorry, but if you won't bite the bullet and get a new drinks machine, we're off.*

GET IT RIGHT! ⭐

In the exam, your response to this task should always be in a fairly formal register, even if you are asked to write for a student audience.

- *My colleagues and I agree that you should appreciate the need to provide us with adequate facilities in order to maximise our efficiency. Regrettably, if you do not invest in a new beverage machine, we will be obliged to withdraw our labour.*

❷ Neither of these statements is perfect – for example, the second one is too long-winded.
- Which is more formal? Which vocabulary and grammar features create this effect?
- Which is more impressively persuasive?

Tone refers to a writer's apparent attitude towards the subject – for example, humorous, angry, critical or passionate. The tone should not change dramatically within a piece of writing, but some variety can be effective. For example, you might use humour, then become more serious.

EXAM FOCUS

Read this part of a successful response to the first task in Question 1. Some features of purpose, audience and form have been highlighted:

> One of my fondest childhood memories is of being photographed with Bobo the chimpanzee in London Zoo. Despite relatives asking 'Which one is you?', the experience probably led to me now sponsoring a family of chimps in the wild. But zoos also contribute to conservation in more immediate ways, such as their extensive breeding programmes for endangered species.

Humour leads to serious point

Formal register and calmly informed tone suggest knowledge

Affectionate personal tone, but still uses formal Standard English

APPLYING YOUR SKILLS

❸ Identify the purpose, audience and form in the following task. Then write the first three sentences of a response.

'It is all too easy to sign an online petition for a good cause and feel you are "doing your bit" for social change, when in fact you are just easing your conscience.'

Write an entry for a blog focusing on social media in which you explain your views on this statement.

Remember:

- Write appropriately for your purpose, audience and form.
- Choose the right tone and register.

KEY FEATURES OF NON-FICTION TEXTS EXPRESSING A VIEWPOINT

WHAT LANGUAGE TECHNIQUES ARE EFFECTIVE IN EXPRESSING A VIEWPOINT?

PAPER 2, SECTION B

RHETORICAL DEVICES

Rhetorical devices are language techniques used for effect, especially to persuade. The table below outlines some useful rhetorical devices.

Device	Explanation	Example
Tricolon (triple, triad)	Using three words or phrases in a row, often with the most powerful coming last	*... a policy that is uninformed, ineffective, and irresponsible*
Rhetorical question	Question making a point rather than seeking an answer	*Do they think we're complete idiots?*
Alliteration	Repeated use of consonant sounds, especially at the start of words; often used with the tricolon	*The rainforest is difficult, dangerous and often deadly.*
Parallelism	Achieving contrast by repeating a grammatical form	*Zoos claim to provide a lasting refuge for endangered species; all they really offer is a fleeting distraction for bored spectators.*

❶ Look at the exam-style task below.

'Fashion is just manufacturers exploiting the insecurity of shoppers, especially the young.'

Write an article for a youth-market magazine expressing your views on this subject.

Write a paragraph from the article in which you agree or disagree with the statement. Try to use all four devices from the table. Add other sentences in between if you wish.

PROVIDING EVIDENCE

To help persuade readers to accept your viewpoint, you should provide evidence. You could combine this with information that shows how you are qualified to speak on the subject. Evidence can take several forms:

● **Anecdote** – a very short story. For example: *'The last time I visited a zoo, a female gorilla very deliberately turned her back on me. I felt ashamed ...'*. (Anecdotes are often a good way to begin.)

- Referring to a study, or to other more informal 'research'. For example: *'A study published in 2015 found that ...'* or *'Many students I have spoken to say that ...'.*
- Statistics (can be used as evidence or for effect in reference to a study) – *'A shocking 59 per cent of prisoners serving sentences of under a year reoffend.'*
- References to the sources in Section A of the exam paper.

TOP TIP

It is fine to make up believable statistics to support your argument, but do not overload your response with them.

❷ Write a short anecdote that you could use when responding to the exam-style task in Question 1.

EXAM FOCUS

Read this part of a successful response to Question 1. Some of the techniques have been highlighted. What others can you find?

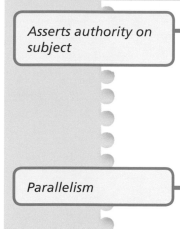

Asserts authority on subject

As a teenager, I know how important image is to young people. Personally, the first thing I notice about someone at a party is what they are wearing. But does this mean that all teenagers are slavish followers of fashion, shallow, empty-headed and vain? Perhaps. At least, that's what psychologists say: we think we're expressing our individuality; actually we're displaying our insecurity.

First-hand evidence

Alliteration

Parallelism

DIRECT APPEALS AND CALLS TO ACTION

Some persuasive texts have very clear objectives. They might be:

- Encouraging people to report bullying
- Making people buy beauty products
- Asking people to donate to a charity

Texts like this may make direct appeals to the reader or urge them to take a particular action. For example:

- *Don't let animals like Flossy suffer needlessly: donate £5 now to ...*

TOP TIP

Use rhetorical devices sparingly. If you use them too frequently, especially one particular device, readers will feel you are trying to manipulate them.

APPLYING YOUR SKILLS

❸ Write the opening paragraph in response to the exam-style task in Question 1. Use the three language techniques covered in this unit to explain your viewpoint.

Remember:

- Use rhetorical devices sparingly – do not overuse any one device.
- Try to provide evidence in some form.
- Speak directly to the reader if it seems appropriate.

USING LANGUAGE TO ARGUE OR PERSUADE

HOW CAN LANGUAGE TECHNIQUES STRENGTHEN AN ARGUMENT?

A05

PAPER 2, SECTION B

Some persuasive writing presents a reasoned argument, often using rhetorical devices. Other texts support their argument with an appeal to the reader's imagination and emotions, using **figurative** and **emotive language**.

FIGURATIVE LANGUAGE

Remind yourself about **figurative language** by looking back at pages 26–9.

❶ **Simile**, **metaphor** and **personification** are all examples of figurative language that can be used to express a critical judgement. Which technique is used in each of the following? What effect does it have?

- *The economy is drifting like a boat with no rudder.*
- *An unenforceable law is as much use as a chocolate teapot.*
- *Some climb the rope ladder of education to success.*
- *War chews up the poor and spits them out.*

❷ Copy and complete the following sentences using figurative language.

- *School pupils all in their identical uniforms, like ... (simile)*
- *She took to the job as easily as a ... (simile)*
- *The ... of opportunity opened and I ... (metaphor)*
- *The steady ... of progress has transformed this community (personification)*

EMOTIVE LANGUAGE

Emotive language aims to create a particular emotional response in readers. For example:

- *Mine closures ripped the heart out of our community.* (strong physical metaphor)
- *Workmen used a chainsaw to hack off ...* (visual detail and **onomatopoeia**)
- *Thanks to your help, vulnerable baby elephants like Bertha can look forward to happy lives.* (adjectives and humanisation of 'Bertha' appeal to our sympathies)

❸ Rewrite these sentences using emotive language for persuasive effect.

- *This unnecessary new road will go through some nice countryside.* (Imply that this will cause serious environmental damage.)
- *Many poorly qualified school-leavers find themselves unemployed.* (Imply that their talents will be wasted.)

TOP TIP

Too much emotive language may alienate your reader ('The road will gouge a trail of brutal carnage through the delicate web of this magical ecosystem.'). Use it carefully.

EXAM FOCUS

Read this extract from a student's essay on unemployment. Some examples of figurative and emotive language have been highlighted:

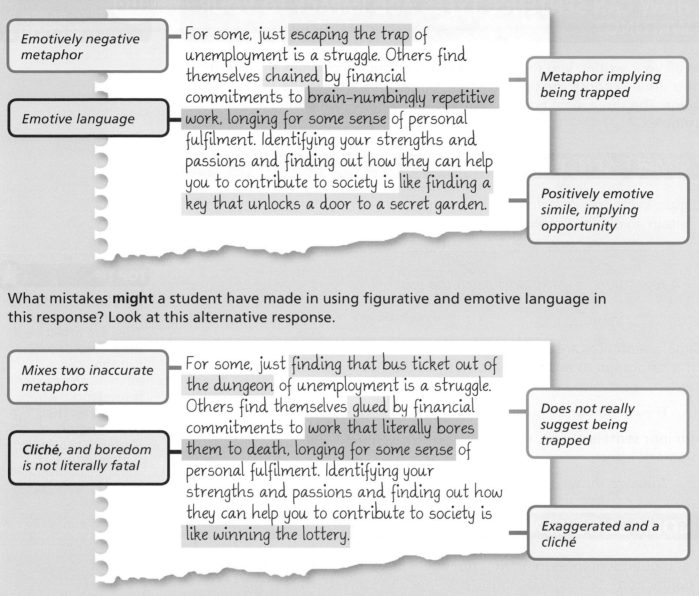

Emotively negative metaphor

Emotive language

For some, just escaping the trap of unemployment is a struggle. Others find themselves chained by financial commitments to brain-numbingly repetitive work, longing for some sense of personal fulfilment. Identifying your strengths and passions and finding out how they can help you to contribute to society is like finding a key that unlocks a door to a secret garden.

Metaphor implying being trapped

Positively emotive simile, implying opportunity

What mistakes **might** a student have made in using figurative and emotive language in this response? Look at this alternative response.

Mixes two inaccurate metaphors

Cliché, and boredom is not literally fatal

For some, just finding that bus ticket out of the dungeon of unemployment is a struggle. Others find themselves glued by financial commitments to work that literally bores them to death, longing for some sense of personal fulfilment. Identifying your strengths and passions and finding out how they can help you to contribute to society is like winning the lottery.

Does not really suggest being trapped

Exaggerated and a cliché

APPLYING YOUR SKILLS

❹   Write at least one persuasive paragraph that uses some figurative and emotive language to argue a case for or against one of the following:

● Lowering the voting age to 16
● Re-legalising fox-hunting
● Introducing a tax on sugary foods

Remember:

● Use a mixture of types of figurative language – simile, metaphor and personification.
● Choose suitable emotive words and phrases, but use them sparingly.

PROGRESS LOG [tick the correct box]   Needs more work ■   Getting there ■   Under control ■

USING DIFFERENT TYPES OF SENTENCES

HOW CAN SENTENCE TYPES ADD IMPACT TO YOUR WRITING?

PAPER 2, SECTION B

In all your writing you should use a variety of sentence types and lengths. You should choose the sentence type carefully to achieve the effect you want. The three main types of sentence are **simple**, **compound** and **complex**.

SIMPLE SENTENCES

Simple sentences contain only a subject and a verb. Sometimes they also contain an object. For example:

A few students walk. Most catch the bus.

Simple sentences are usually short. You can use them effectively at the start of a paragraph to make a point that you then go on to develop. Simple sentences can also be used for dramatic effect. For example:

They need our help. No one else cares.

A **minor sentence**, which is grammatically incomplete, can also achieve dramatic effect:

*They are throwing away their lives. **For nothing.***

> **TOP TIP**
>
> Only use minor sentences rarely. They are effective if used once or twice, but they can alienate the reader if used more often. Remember that overusing any sentence type will lead to dull and repetitive writing.

COMPOUND SENTENCES

Compound sentences join two simple sentences using a **coordinating conjunction**, such as 'and', 'but', 'or' , 'nor', 'so' or 'yet'. For example:

- *They know what they want **and** will do anything to get it.*
- *We work hard, **yet** we remain unrecognised.*
- *Relationships are a compromise, **so** we have to make sacrifices.*

COMPLEX (SUBORDINATED) SENTENCES

Complex sentences include a **main clause** that makes sense on its own, and at least one **subordinate clause** that only makes sense in relation to the main clause.

❶ Identify the main clause and the subordinate clause in each of the following sentences:
- *Owain, although he lives in Wales, plays for England.*
- *Having been brought up in the UK, they are completely bilingual.*
- *Switzerland, which is advanced in many ways, gave women the vote only in 1990.*

EXAM FOCUS

Read this extract from a student's response showing a variety of sentence types to express a viewpoint:

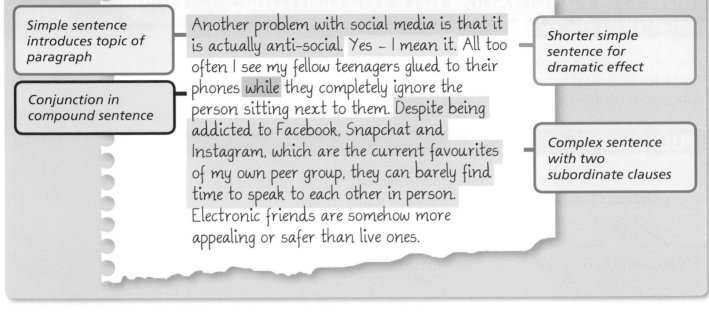

Simple sentence introduces topic of paragraph

Conjunction in compound sentence

Another problem with social media is that it is actually anti-social. Yes – I mean it. All too often I see my fellow teenagers glued to their phones while they completely ignore the person sitting next to them. Despite being addicted to Facebook, Snapchat and Instagram, which are the current favourites of my own peer group, they can barely find time to speak to each other in person. Electronic friends are somehow more appealing or safer than live ones.

Shorter simple sentence for dramatic effect

Complex sentence with two subordinate clauses

What mistakes **might** a student have made here?

- They might have started with a long, complex sentence, and lost the reader's interest.
- They might have used two or three very short sentences, losing impact.
- They might have overloaded the complex sentence with more subordinate clauses, making it confusing.
- They might have ended the paragraph with a long, complex sentence instead of a shorter one that makes an effective concluding point.

TOP TIP

Addressing or questioning the reader directly can be effective: 'Take a close look. Is he really what he seems?'

APPLYING YOUR SKILLS

❷ Rewrite the passage below using a variety of sentence lengths and types for effect.

Social media apps are the new social glue. We used to be limited to face-to-face communication. Now we can talk to each other in many ways. We can invite all our friends to a party on Facebook in seconds. Facebook is very easy to use. Even my granddad uses it. Some people talk about the threat of social media. They point to cyber-bullying. They also say it is used by terrorists. Any form of communication can be used for good or bad. The internet is a way to join our intelligences. We become one huge interconnected human mind. This could be the way forward for humanity.

Remember:

- Use all three types of sentence: simple, compound and complex.
- Start or end with a short, simple sentence for effect.
- Use a minor sentence if it will create impact.
- Avoid overloading complex sentence with lots of subordinate clauses.

PROGRESS LOG [tick the correct box]   Needs more work ☐   Getting there ☐   Under control ☐

USING PUNCTUATION TO PERSUADE

HOW CAN PUNCTUATION HELP YOU GET YOUR MEANING ACROSS?

A06

PAPER 2, SECTION B

You can make your persuasive sentences even more effective – and earn marks for technical accuracy – by using a range of punctuation. Using punctuation correctly and creatively is important for clarifying your ideas.

FULL STOPS

A sentence usually ends with a full stop. Remember that all sentences (except **minor sentences** for effect) must have a subject and a verb:

Subject

Cars pollute. They are noisy. They squash hedgehogs.

Verb

COMMAS TO CLARIFY

Commas divide clauses in order to make the meaning instantly clear. They allow you to write sentences that will not confuse your reader:

> *WhatsApp, which enables 'group chat', works on wi-fi, avoiding the need for a mobile signal.*

You also need commas in lists, which can give your writing a sense of plenty and variety:

> *You can get anything you want online: from socks, sweatshirts, baseball caps and cheerleader jackets, to iPhones, selfie-sticks and frozen pizzas.*

Look at how the commas in these sentences make them more persuasive:

- *People should learn more languages: it is useful to speak Punjabi, Welsh is spoken in Snowdonia, and Belgium uses French and Flemish.*

- *Dedication is the key: after eating, Sammy, Elva and Gil always practise.*

❶ Punctuate these sentences:

- *Although many apps are free downloading them uses up your data*

- *It is free simple to use and readily available and what's more it works*

DASHES AND PARENTHESES

Clauses can also be divided with **dashes** or **round brackets** (like these):

- *Marmite – you either love it or loathe it – apparently divides the world.*

- *You can even buy vegetarian black sausage – though why you'd want to beats me.*

> **TOP TIP** ⭐
>
> Avoid commas that do nothing to change or clarify meaning. For example, this sentence does not need any commas: 'My friend Pam the plumber could fix that tap for you in ten minutes if you paid her.'

Use a dash to add drama, humour or to suggest that information is interesting but not essential. This effect is slightly stronger with parentheses:

> *Actors like Jennifer Lawrence and Kit Harington (tipped for a BAFTA) show that it is possible to combine drama and psychological insight.*

SEMICOLONS AND COLONS

The **semicolon** (;) and **colon** (:) are useful in viewpoint writing (see pages 12–13):

- *Friendship can be temporary; parenting lasts a lifetime.*
- *There is only one reason to take a bus: the price.*

QUESTION AND EXCLAMATION MARKS

Use a question mark with every question, even a **rhetorical** one. Use exclamation marks sparingly for a surprising, amusing or ironic point:

> *And why do we wear uniform? To make us feel we belong!*

GET IT RIGHT! ⭐

Never use more than one exclamation mark at a time!

EXAM FOCUS

Read this response to see how a student has used punctuation:

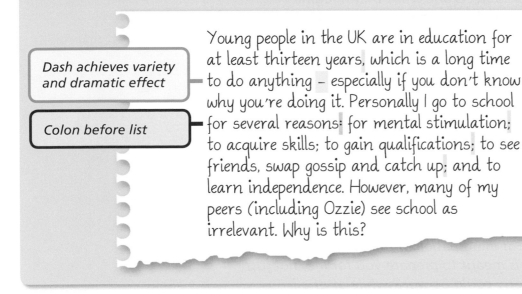

Dash achieves variety and dramatic effect

Colon before list

> Young people in the UK are in education for at least thirteen years, which is a long time to do anything – especially if you don't know why you're doing it. Personally I go to school for several reasons: for mental stimulation; to acquire skills; to gain qualifications; to see friends, swap gossip and catch up; and to learn independence. However, many of my peers (including Ozzie) see school as irrelevant. Why is this?

Comma before subordinate clause

Semicolons enable list within a list

❷ How is punctuation used in the final two sentences above?

APPLYING YOUR SKILLS

❸ Write a paragraph on cyber-bullying and how to deal with it. Use the punctuation techniques outlined in this unit.

Remember:

- Use commas to clarify.
- Use dashes and round brackets to divide clauses effectively.
- Use colons and semicolons to divide ideas.

PROGRESS LOG [tick the correct box]   Needs more work ▪   Getting there ▪   Under control ▪

USING STRUCTURES CREATIVELY

HOW CAN STRUCTURE CONVEY YOUR MESSAGE?

A05

PAPER 2,
SECTION B

In your exam, you will receive marks for developing your ideas in each paragraph and throughout your whole response.

STRUCTURE WITHIN PARAGRAPHS

Effective paragraphs usually:

- Focus on one central idea each
- Begin with a **topic sentence**
- Show a progression of ideas
- Use **connectives** to link ideas

For example:

Topic sentence   Development of topic sentence

*Many students see education as irrelevant. **They fail to see a connection between school subjects and what they imagine themselves doing in the future.** **For example,** if you plan to be an engineer, studying poetry may seem pointless ...*

Linking phrase

Example

There is no single correct way to structure a paragraph, but you should try to show a progression of ideas, enhanced by your choice of sentence types, and using linking words and phrases to show the relationship between ideas.

Look at these sentences, which develop the paragraph above:

Introduces argument opposing previous idea
(that studying poetry is pointless)

*However, **this shows a lack of imagination in thinking about the purpose of education. If it is meant to prepare you for life, not just for a job, then perhaps poetry could be worthwhile after all.***

Explains why it shows a 'lack of imagination'

CONNECTIVES

Connectives (such as 'although' and 'moreover') are words and phrases that link ideas and prepare readers for each new development. Connectives help to shape the whole paragraph. In the example above, 'However' prepares the reader for a contradiction of the view that poetry is pointless for engineers.

❶ Write a topic sentence for a paragraph suggesting that schools should focus more on verbal than written communication skills. Then continue the paragraph, using at least two connectives and building to a concluding point.

EXAM FOCUS

Read this paragraph and the notes on how it is structured:

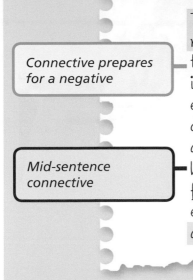

Compelling start

Connective prepares for a negative

The jarring buzz of the bell jolts me out of my thoughts, and I gather up my books for the next lesson – history. Unfortunately, this is at the other end of the school and everyone else is streaming in the opposite direction. Before long, the bell sounds again, and it's maths. My head is still in the Second World War, yet the teacher expects me to focus on algebra. Much as I try, the numbers escape me. My whole day is like this: chaotic and disjointed.

Mid-sentence connective

Draws conclusion

OVERALL STRUCTURE

Your writing should always have a clear overall structure. You should plan this out before you start writing, but be prepared to adapt your plan if you have better ideas as you write.

Here is a possible structure for a task asking you to write about the value of education.

(1) Start by introducing the subject. You could get the reader's attention with:

- An **anecdote** (as in the Exam Focus box)
- A quotation: *'Education is not preparation for life; education is life itself.'* (John Dewey)
- A statistic: *'Over 70 per cent of school leavers ...'*
- A controversial claim: *'Secondary schools exist to keep teenagers out of their parents' way and off the streets until they are old enough to do something useful.'*

(2) Then explain its significance, perhaps raising questions to be addressed.

Two or three paragraphs **explaining the problem** and **arguing for a solution** – for example, proposing that schools should have whole-morning lessons.

(3) Now add a paragraph considering at least one **alternative viewpoint** – such as that teenagers get bored easily.

(4) End with a **conclusion** dismissing opposing arguments, perhaps weighing them up ('On balance ...'), drawing ideas together and leaving readers with a memorable message.

TOP TIP

Vary your paragraph structure by using some connectives mid-sentence: 'Rocket science is clearly a specialist subject. Education, *on the other hand*, is a subject everyone thinks they know about.'

APPLYING YOUR SKILLS

❷ Write a plan for a response to this task:

'Studying history in school is a waste of time. Pupils should be learning skills that focus on the here and now in modern Britain.'

Write a letter to your school governors explaining your views on this claim.

❸ Now write an engaging opening paragraph and a concluding paragraph based on your plan.

Remember:

- Your plan should reflect a development of ideas.
- Use connectives in your paragraph.
- Get your reader's attention, and end with a compelling statement.

PROGRESS CHECK FOR CHAPTER 5

GOOD PROGRESS

I can:

- Write in an appropriate register for purpose, audience and form ☐
- Use a range of language techniques and punctuation ☐
- Plan a structured response ☐

EXCELLENT PROGRESS

I can:

- Write in a consistent and appropriate tone for a purpose ☐
- Use figurative and emotive language persuasively ☐
- Use sentence types and punctuation in varied and creative ways ☐

CHAPTER 6: GCSE English Language practice papers

INTRODUCTION

The practice papers in this chapter are designed to be as similar as possible to those that you will face in the real exam. You can use them for exam practice by writing answers in note form, or you can use them as extra mock exams, writing full answers as you would in the exam and timing yourself following the guidance given below. Check the answers in the back of the book against what you have written.

Time allowed: 1 hour 45 minutes for each paper. It is suggested below how you could divide the time allowed between Sections A and B.

PAPER 1

SECTION A

Timing: about an hour, including planning

Marks: 40 out of a total of 80 for the paper

Assessment objectives: Q1 AO1, Q2 AO2, Q3 AO2, Q4 AO4

SECTION B

Timing: 45 minutes, including planning

Marks: 40 (24 for content and organisation; 16 for spelling, punctuation and grammar) out of a total of 80 for the paper

Assessment objectives: Q5 AO5, AO6

PAPER 2

SECTION A

Timing: about an hour, including planning

Marks: 40 out of a total of 80 for the paper

Assessment objectives: Q1 AO1, Q2 AO1, Q3 AO2, Q4 AO3

SECTION B

Timing: 45 minutes, including planning

Marks: 40 (24 for content and organisation; 16 for spelling, punctuation and grammar) out of a total of 80 for the paper

Assessment objectives: Q5 AO5, AO6

PAPER 1: EXPLORATIONS IN CREATIVE READING AND WRITING

SOURCE A

This extract is from the opening of a short story by H. G. Wells. A medical scientist is showing a visitor his laboratory in London.

'The Stolen Bacillus'

'This again,' said the Bacteriologist, slipping a glass slide under the microscope, 'is well, – a preparation of the Bacillus of cholera – the cholera germ.'

The pale-faced man peered down the microscope. He was evidently not accustomed to that kind of thing, and held a limp white hand over his disengaged eye. 'I see very
5   little,' he said.

'Touch this screw,' said the Bacteriologist; 'perhaps the microscope is out of focus for you. Eyes vary so much. Just the fraction of a turn this way or that.'

'Ah! now I see,' said the visitor. 'Not so very much to see after all. Little streaks and shreds of pink. And yet those little particles, those mere atomies, might multiply and
10   devastate a city! Wonderful!'

He stood up, and releasing the glass slip from the microscope, held it in his hand towards the window. 'Scarcely visible,' he said, scrutinising the preparation. He hesitated. 'Are these – alive? Are they dangerous now?'

'Those have been stained and killed,' said the Bacteriologist. 'I wish, for my own part,
15   we could kill and stain every one of them in the universe.'

'I suppose,' the pale man said, with a slight smile, 'that you scarcely care to have such things about you in the living – in the active state?'

'On the contrary, we are obliged to,' said the Bacteriologist. 'Here, for instance –' He walked across the room and took up one of several sealed tubes. 'Here is the living
20   thing. This is a cultivation of the actual living disease bacteria.' He hesitated. 'Bottled cholera, so to speak.'

A slight gleam of satisfaction appeared momentarily in the face of the pale man. 'It's a deadly thing to have in your possession,' he said, devouring the little tube with his eyes. The Bacteriologist watched the morbid pleasure in his visitor's expression. This
25   man, who had visited him that afternoon with a note of introduction from an old friend, interested him from the very contrast of their dispositions. The lank black hair and deep grey eyes, the haggard expression and nervous manner, the fitful yet keen interest of his visitor were a novel change from the phlegmatic[1] deliberations of the ordinary scientific worker with whom the Bacteriologist chiefly associated. It was
30   perhaps natural, with a hearer evidently so impressionable to the lethal nature of his topic, to take the most effective aspect of the matter.

35 He held the tube in his hand thoughtfully. 'Yes, here is the pestilence imprisoned. Only break such a little tube as this into a supply of drinking-water, say to these minute particles of life that one must needs stain and examine with the highest powers of the microscope even to see, and that one can neither smell nor taste – say to them, "Go forth, increase and multiply, and replenish the cisterns,"[2] and death – mysterious, untraceable death, death swift and terrible, death full of pain and indignity – would be released upon this city, and go hither and thither seeking his victims. Here he would take the husband from the wife, here the child from its

40 mother, here the statesman from his duty, and here the toiler from his trouble. He would follow the water-mains, creeping along streets, picking out and punishing a house here and a house there where they did not boil their drinking-water, creeping into the wells of the mineral water makers, getting washed into salad, and lying dormant in ices. He would wait ready to be drunk in the horse-troughs, and by

45 unwary children in the public fountains. He would soak into the soil, to reappear in springs and wells at a thousand unexpected places. Once start him at the water supply, and before we could ring him in, and catch him again, he would have decimated the metropolis.'[3]

Glossary:
[1] *phlegmatic* – unemotional, calm, down to earth
[2] *cisterns* – water storage tanks
[3] *decimated the metropolis* – killed everyone in London

SECTION A: READING

Answer **all** questions in this section.

You are advised to spend about 45 minutes on this section.

❶ Read again the first four paragraphs of the source.

List **four** things from this part of the source about the visitor.

[4 marks]

❷ Look in detail at this extract from lines 16–32 of the source:

'I suppose,' the pale man said, with a slight smile, 'that you scarcely care to have such things about you in the living – in the active state?'

'On the contrary, we are obliged to,' said the Bacteriologist. 'Here, for instance –' He walked across the room and took up one of several sealed tubes. 'Here is the living thing. This is a cultivation of the actual living disease bacteria.' He hesitated. 'Bottled cholera, so to speak.'

A slight gleam of satisfaction appeared momentarily in the face of the pale man. 'It's a deadly thing to have in your possession,' he said, devouring the little tube with his eyes. The Bacteriologist watched the morbid pleasure in his visitor's expression. This man, who had visited him that afternoon with a note of introduction from an old friend, interested him from the very contrast of their dispositions. The lank black hair and deep grey eyes, the haggard expression and nervous manner, the fitful yet keen interest of his visitor were a novel change from the phlegmatic[1] deliberations of the ordinary scientific worker with whom the Bacteriologist chiefly associated. It was perhaps natural, with a hearer evidently so impressionable to the lethal nature of his topic, to take the most effective aspect of the matter.

How does the writer use language here to describe the visitor?

You could comment on the writer's choice of:

● Words and phrases

● Language features and techniques

● Sentence forms

[8 marks]

❸ You now need to think about the **whole** of the **source**.
This text is the opening of a story.

How has the writer structured the text to interest you as a reader?
You could write about:

● What the writer focuses your attention on at the beginning

● How and why the writer changes this focus as the source develops

● Any other structural features that interest you

[8 marks]

❹ Now look at the last part of the source, from line 33 to the end.

A student, having read this section of the text said: 'The writer is very effective in bringing to life the threat of the bacillus and the bacteriologist's attitude towards it.'

To what extent do you agree?

In your response, you could:

● Write about your own impressions of the bacillus and the bacteriologist

● Evaluate how the writer has created these impressions

● Support your opinions with references to the text

[20 marks]

SECTION B: WRITING

You are advised to spend about 45 minutes on this section.

Write in full sentences.

You are reminded of the need to plan your answer.

You should leave enough time to check your work at the end.

❺ You are going to enter a creative writing competition.

Either: Write a description suggested by this picture:

Or: Write a story about a scientific experiment that goes wrong.

(24 marks for content and organisation
16 marks for technical accuracy)

[40 marks]

PROGRESS LOG [tick the correct box]   Needs more work ☐   Getting there ☐   Under control ☐

PAPER 2: WRITERS' VIEWPOINTS AND PERSPECTIVES

SOURCE A

Fashion Goes Pop

Alice Fisher, *The Guardian*, **20 March 2011 (theguardian.com)**

Spring is a fertile time. Not just for the lambs and the budding trees, but for fashion and trends. The first months of each year bring the latest round of catwalk shows from New York, London, Milan and Paris, and the concurrent awards season sent the best dressed in film and music trotting up the red carpets to the Grammys,
5 the Brits, the Baftas and the Oscars. Spring is an orgy of style.

In the old days, if you wanted to look at the beautifully ridiculous, the conceptual or the just plain silly, the fashion shows were your best bet. Awards ceremonies, by contrast, used to be elegant oceans of pretty, colourful gowns by Valentino, Marchesa and Versace. They were so sedate that, in 2001, when Björk wore a swan
10 dress by fashion designer Marjan Pejoski and laid six eggs on the red carpet at the Oscars, she was lampooned for years. In 2011, a decade later, nobody would blink if Björk had taken off and flown to her seat. This spring, at the Grammys, Katy Perry sported angel wings, 10-year-old actress and pop star Willow Smith turned up in 8in platform trainers, US singer Nicki Minaj added leopard-print highlights to her
15 pompadour[1] hair to match her leopard-print dress and Lady Gaga arrived in an egg, carried like a Roman emperor.

The designers' most outrageous creations were papped[2] on celebrities at red-carpet events rather than at the fashion shows. In fact, the most talked-about turn on the catwalk this season wasn't by Kate Moss, Lara Stone or any other model – it was
20 Lady Gaga's debut at the Thierry Mugler womenswear show in Paris. Something odd is happening with celebrities and style. The stars are becoming more daring, more avant garde than the designers.

Nowadays, the biggest female names in music don't particularly set themselves apart from their predecessors through musical style – most of them create
25 surprisingly traditional pop – but the way they look is a whole new world ...

The new stars do seem to be more humorous and self-aware than their pop predecessors. When Jessie J won the Critics' Choice at this year's Brit Awards she wore a Vivienne Westwood minidress. 'I look like the evil queen from *Snow White*,' she told reporters. 'I just need to go and find my dwarfs now.' Similarly, when asked
30 about her big-cat Givenchy couture[3] at this year's Grammys, Minaj described her outfit as 'miraculous meets her cub meets ferocity meets fabulosity meets the runway'. Katy Perry is more pragmatic. 'We're all unique. That's why we all win and we all can exist. People don't just want vanilla. They want 31 flavours. I couldn't do what Rihanna does. I couldn't do what Gaga does. They can't do what I do.'

35 What these stars do is create a break in the monotony of style that has smothered culture of late. Trends used to wash from catwalk to stage to club and pavement unhampered. They may not be of vast cultural significance, but these new celebrities' style is vivid and fun. We have come a long way from laughing at a star for laying eggs on a red carpet to applauding one for arriving in an egg. It's going

40 to be entertaining to see how much further we can go.

Glossary:

pompadour[1] – a hairstyle in which the hair is brushed upwards for height

papped[2] – photographed by paparazzi (independent photographers who take pictures of celebrities)

couture[3] – fashionable made-to-measure clothing

SOURCE B

Letter from George Bernard Shaw to *The Times* 3 July 1905

Sir, The Opera management of Covent Garden regulates the dress of its male patrons. When is it going to do the same to the women?

On Saturday night I went to the Opera. I wore the costume imposed on me by the regulations of the house. I fully recognize the advantage of those regulations.

5 Evening dress is cheap, simple, durable, prevents rivalry and extravagance on the part of male leaders of fashion, annihilates class distinctions and gives men who are poor and doubtful of their social position (that is, the great majority of men) a sense of security and satisfaction that no clothes of their own choosing could confer ...

10 But I submit that what is sauce for the gander is sauce for the goose. Every argument that applies to the regulation of the man's dress applies equally to the regulation of the woman's. ...

At 9 o'clock (the Opera began at 8) a lady came in and sat down very conspicuously in my line of sight. She remained there until the beginning of the last act. I do not

15 complain of her coming late and going early; on the contrary, I wish she had come later and gone earlier. For this lady, who had very black hair, had stuck over her right ear the pitiable corpse of a large white bird, which looked exactly if someone had killed it by stamping on the beast, and then nailed it to the lady's temple, which was presumably of sufficient solidity to bear the operation.

20 I am not, I hope, a morbidly squeamish person; but the spectacle sickened me. I presume that if I had presented myself at the doors with a dead snake round my neck, a collection of black beetles pinned to my shirtfront, and a grouse in my hair, I should have been refused admission. Why, then, is a woman to be allowed to commit such a public outrage? Had the lady been refused admission, as she should

25 have been, she would have soundly rated the tradesman who imposed the disgusting headdress on her under the false pretence that 'the best people' wear such things, and withdrawn her custom from him; and thus the root of the evil

30 would be struck at; for your fashionable woman generally allows herself to be dressed according to the taste of a person who she would not let sit down in her presence. I once, in Drury Lane Theatre, sat behind a matinee hat decorated with the two wings of a seagull, artificially reddened at the joints so as to produce the illusion of being freshly plucked from a live bird. But even that lady stopped short of a whole seagull. Both ladies were evidently regarded by their neighbours as ridiculous and vulgar; but that is hardly enough when the offence is one which

35 produces a sensation of physical sickness in persons of normal human sensibility.

I suggest to the Covent Garden authorities that, if they feel bound to protect their subscribers against the dangers of my shocking them with a blue tie, they are at least equally bound to protect me against the danger of a woman shocking me with a dead bird.

Yours truly,
    G. Bernard Shaw

SECTION A: READING

Answer **all** questions in this section.

You are advised to spend about 45 minutes on this section.

❶ Read again the first two paragraphs of **Source A**.

Choose **four** statements below which are TRUE. Choose a maximum of four statements.

[4 marks]

A Fashion shows take place in large cities.

B The Brits and the Baftas are fashion shows.

C The writer thinks that modern fashion shows are ridiculous.

D Marchesa is a fashion designer.

E Björk was once ridiculed for one of her outfits.

F The writer thinks that celebrities wear boring outfits at awards ceremonies.

G Katy Perry wore angel wings to an awards ceremony.

H Modern audiences are surprised when celebrities wear outrageous costumes.

❷ You need to refer to **Source A** and **Source B** for this question:

Use details from **both** sources. Write a summary of the differences in attitudes to fashion in the two articles.

[8 marks]

❸ You now need to refer **only** to **Source B**, Shaw's letter.

How does Shaw use language to express his views on fashion persuasively?

[12 marks]

❹ For this question, you need to refer to the **whole of Source A** together with **Source B**, the letter to *The Times*.

Compare how the two writers convey their different attitudes to fashion.

In your answer, you could:

- Compare their different attitudes
- Compare the methods they use to convey their attitudes
- Support your ideas with references to both texts   **[16 marks]**

SECTION B: WRITING

You are advised to spend about 45 minutes on this section.

Write in full sentences.

You are reminded of the need to plan your answer.

You should leave enough time to check your work at the end.

❺ 'Clothes are not just functional – they are an essential way in which we express our individuality.'

Write an article for a broadsheet newspaper in which you explain your views on this statement.

(24 marks for content and organisation
16 marks for technical accuracy)

[40 marks]

PROGRESS LOG [tick the correct box]   Needs more work ☐   Getting there ☐   Under control ☐

CHAPTER 7: The basics: Core Literature skills and effects

HOW TO COMMENT ON TEXTS AND USE QUOTATIONS (A01) (A02)

When commenting on a text in your Literature exam, you should always support what you say with references or by using quotations effectively.

USING QUOTATIONS

Using quotations accurately can make your answer more sophisticated. Remember:

- Always use single quotation marks (' ') around the quotation.
- Only put quotation marks around words taken from the text.
- Embed the quotation into the sentence, so that it flows easily when read.
- Do not use a quotation and then repeat what it means in your own words.
- Do not overuse quotations. Use them to support the most important points.

EXAM FOCUS

Read this part of a student's response to a task on the character of Admiral Greystock in Anthony Trollope's novel *The Eustace Diamonds.* Some of its features have been highlighted:

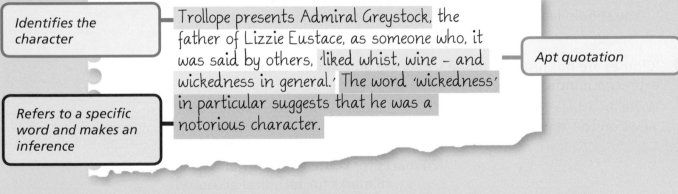

Identifies the character

Trollope presents Admiral Greystock, the father of Lizzie Eustace, as someone who, it was said by others, 'liked whist, wine – and wickedness in general.' The word 'wickedness' in particular suggests that he was a notorious character.

Apt quotation

Refers to a specific word and makes an inference

A higher-level response would explore the point further, focusing on particular words and their effect to identify further implications:

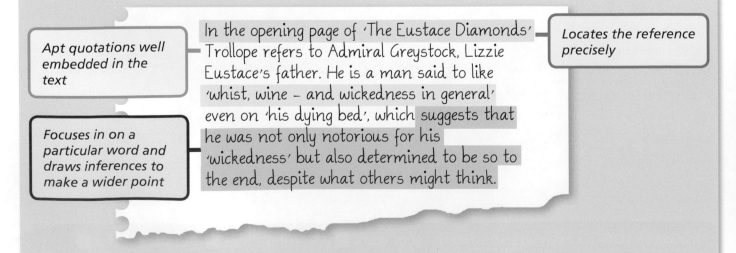

Apt quotations well embedded in the text

In the opening page of 'The Eustace Diamonds' Trollope refers to Admiral Greystock, Lizzie Eustace's father. He is a man said to like 'whist, wine – and wickedness in general' even on 'his dying bed', which suggests that he was not only notorious for his 'wickedness' but also determined to be so to the end, despite what others might think.

Locates the reference precisely

Focuses in on a particular word and draws inferences to make a wider point

❶ Rewrite this comment on Meera Syal's novel *Anita and Me* as a single sentence, embedding the quotation.

Meena describes how the Tollington women show their mutual dislike of each other. They 'snarl and send death rays to each other'.

DEVELOP A CRITICAL STYLE

The style in which you write your interpretation of a text is important. In AO1 you are asked to write in a critical style.

What does it say?	What does it mean?	Dos and Don'ts
AO1 'maintain a critical style'	Write in a clear, formal style using **Standard English**, not in a chatty, informal style.	**Don't write:** *What the writer is sort of going on about is …* **Do write:** *The writer is making the underlying point that …*

When writing in a critical style, you should use a range of verbs to show the effects created in the text:

- *The writer presents/suggests/conveys/implies/explores/describes/demonstrates/reveals …*
- *The reader/audience infers/understands/recognises/perceives/deduces …*

❷ Choose alternative verbs to replace the underlined verbs.
- *The author **says** that the main character …*
- *In this scene Shakespeare **shows** …*
- *As events unfold, the audience **can tell** …*
- *The sense of fear is **shown** by …*

PLAN YOUR RESPONSE

Remember to write your response in paragraphs and to use **connectives**. You should plan for about six or seven paragraphs. Always include:

- An introduction: outline the main point or argument you will make
- A conclusion: sum up your argument (you could begin: 'Finally …')

> **TOP TIP** ⭐
>
> You can also make references without quotations to support a point, e.g. *In the first chapter the writer presents us with each main character, which allows the reader to gain an overall impression of them.*

> **TOP TIP** ⭐
>
> Once you are sure you understand the question, plan your answer quickly. List key ideas. Note down important names, places and key events.

APPLYING YOUR SKILLS

❸ Reread a section from the text you are studying when a key character appears for the first time. Write 100 words commenting on that character.

Remember:

- Comment on what you learn about the character from their first appearance.
- Include short, important quotations.

WRITING ABOUT SETTINGS AND CONTEXTS

The context of any text is:

- The social and historical time, place and conditions in which it was written
- Where and when it is set
- Its literary **genre** – how it relates to similar texts

There are 6 marks out of 30 available for context on each question you answer.

CONTEXT IN SHAKESPEARE

Context is especially important when writing about Shakespeare's plays, because society has changed so much in the 400 years since they were written. Here are some key points about the context in which Shakespeare wrote:

- People believed in the Divine Right of Kings, which meant the monarch was answerable only to God.
- Theatres attracted both the educated rich and the uneducated poor.
- Women had little power. An ambitious woman, like the character of Lady Macbeth, had to channel her ambition through her husband. A young woman, like Juliet in *Romeo and Juliet*, was expected to accept her father's choice of a husband.
- Almost everyone believed in God, and in witchcraft and ghosts, as seen in *Macbeth*.

❶ Make notes on the factors listed above that are particularly relevant to the play you are studying.

CONTEXT IN THE NINETEENTH-CENTURY NOVEL

Here are some key points about the context of nineteenth-century novels:

- Britain's overseas empire made it a major world power.
- Women had few rights and were financially dependent on their husbands.
- The gap between rich and poor was huge. There was no National Health Service.
- Science frequently influenced literature, as can be seen in *Frankenstein*.
- Most people attended church regularly.

❷ Make notes on the circumstances of the main characters in the novel you are studying. Are they affected by any of the factors above? If so, to what extent?

CONTEXT IN MODERN TEXTS

You will find the basic contexts of modern texts quite familiar. However, you should research the specific contexts of your texts. For example:

- *An Inspector Calls* is set just before the First World War, but it was written in 1945, after the Second World War.
- *Animal Farm* satirises the Russian Revolution of 1917 and later developments in Communism.
- *Blood Brothers* reflects Willy Russell's attitude towards the effects of Margaret Thatcher's Conservative government on society in the 1980s.

❸ Find out when the text you are studying was written, when it is set and what historical and social factors might have influenced it.

EXAM FOCUS

Read this comment on context and see why it is successful:

Precisely identifies setting	Meera Syal set 'Anita and Me' in a former mining village in which the only Asian family is the narrator's, but at a time when racism was growing in nearby cities. Anita's admiration for racism is painful to Meena, but helps to develop her as a character.	Identifies relevant developing context
Explains effect of contextual factor		

WHAT ARE SETTING AND ATMOSPHERE AND HOW DO THEY LINK TO MOOD AND TONE?

Setting is an important part of context. It tells the reader where and when the action of a story takes place. For example, part of a story might occur on the River Thames at night, as in *Great Expectations*.

A story may have a number of settings. They help to generate an appropriate **mood** and **tone**. For example, *Jane Eyre* begins on a dismal winter's day. This sets the mood in which the narrator begins to describe her unhappy childhood.

Setting can be linked to **themes**. The 1950s play *A Taste of Honey*, is about a lonely, neglected girl who becomes pregnant. This matches its setting: a rented attic room in a deprived part of Salford, suggesting themes of growing up in poverty, neglect, responsibility and loneliness.

APPLYING YOUR SKILLS

❹ Draw a spider diagram. In the centre write the name of a text you are studying.

Make notes on the diagram about the context of the text and the significance of its settings.

HOW TO WRITE ABOUT CHARACTERS

Writers sometimes simply describe what a character is like – for example, in *A Christmas Carol*, Dickens describes Scrooge as *'solitary as an oyster'*. Modern playwrights may also describe their characters in **stage directions**. Often, however, writers reveal characters in less direct ways. They might do this through:

- Physical appearance or clothing
- Their actions (for example, whether they are kind or cruel)
- What they say, in **dialogue** with other characters, in **soliloquies** (Shakespeare plays) or as first-person narrators
- What other characters say about them

In the exam, you need to comment on characters and support your comments with evidence of this kind.

> **TOP TIP** ⭐
>
> A Shakespeare soliloquy is a **monologue**, as if the character is thinking aloud. It provides a good insight into the character's thoughts.

CHARACTER IN SHAKESPEARE

An exam question about a Shakespeare play is likely to focus on aspects of character. For example:

- How a character's choices affect events
- How characters are affected by events
- The relationship between characters
- How characters develop through their experiences

❶ Write a 100-word commentary on one of Shakespeare's characters. Include:

- A quotation that reflects their character
- What others think of them
- How they affect the plot

> **TOP TIP** ⭐
>
> Make sure you know who narrates the novel you are studying. If there are multiple narrators (as in *Frankenstein*), make a note of the points at which their narrations occur.

NARRATIVE VIEWPOINT AND VOICE IN A NOVEL

In a novel, characters are presented by the narrator or narrators. The **narrative viewpoint** of a novel can be written in the:

- First person – often in the voice of the **protagonist**, as in *Jane Eyre* and *Anita and Me*; the narrator may be unreliable, particularly if they are a child, as in *Pigeon English*

- Third person, narrated directly by the writer, who has complete knowledge of all the characters (as in *Pride and Prejudice*) but who may at times narrate in a voice that is **ironic** or judgemental

- Third person, but mainly focusing on one character's perspective – perhaps just for a part of the novel, with another character coming to the fore later on

EXAM FOCUS

In *Pride and Prejudice*, Mr Collins is a pompous, narrow-minded clergyman. Read one student's comment about how the narrative voice presents him:

> The narrative voice strikes a sharp tone when we are told that 'Mr Collins was not a sensible man' and the reader feels as if the narrator disapproves of him.

— Identifies the mood

— Effect on the reader

Compare this with a student's response about *The Strange Case of Dr Jekyll and Mr Hyde*:

> The third person narrative voice gives us the lawyer Mr Utterson's authoritative point of view. His 'definite presentiment' that Mr Hyde is 'a fiend' sounds a warning and alarms the reader as well as Utterson himself.

— Identifies the type of narrative voice and point of view

— Identifies the mood and effect on the reader

❷ Write a paragraph analysing the effects of narrative viewpoint and voice in a novel. Include an analysis of their effects.

STAGE DIRECTIONS IN DRAMATIC TEXTS

Stage directions can give an impression of a character. In *An Inspector Calls*, the playwright describes Sheila as 'a pretty girl in her early twenties'. Stage directions may even give us an insight into character. Eric, Sheila's brother, is described as 'not quite at ease, half shy, half assertive'.

In drama, characters are revealed through their actions as well as their words. Their actions reflect their **motivation**. For example, in *Blood Brothers*, Mickey agrees to help his brother Sammy take part in a robbery. Mickey has no job and has low self-esteem. He is easily undermined by Sammy, who humiliates him by suggesting he has achieved nothing in life.

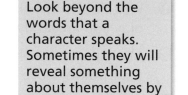

TOP TIP

Look beyond the words that a character speaks. Sometimes they will reveal something about themselves by a look or gesture.

❸ Make notes on the important actions the main characters take in a text you are studying. How do these actions reveal the character?

APPLYING YOUR SKILLS

❹ Write an analysis of one character in a text you are studying.

Remember:

- Include at least one piece of revealing description from the narrator or another character.
- Comment on how the narrative viewpoint affects the presentation of the character.
- Include what the character says and does and what these reveal.

PROGRESS LOG [tick the correct box]   Needs more work ▨   Getting there ▨   Under control ▨

HOW TO WRITE ABOUT THEMES

A **theme** is a central idea that runs through a work of literature. Themes are often connected.

THEMES IN SHAKESPEARE

Shakespeare's themes explore questions about society, politics, morality and relationships, and even his comedies can have serious themes.

Some common themes in Shakespeare's plays are:

- Conflict between parents and children (*Romeo and Juliet*)
- Ambition (*Macbeth*)
- Love, courtship and marriage (*Much Ado About Nothing*)
- Race and the role of women (*The Merchant of Venice*)
- The supernatural (*The Tempest*)
- Power (*Julius Caesar*)

HOW ARE THEMES REVEALED IN THE PLAYS?

Themes can be revealed through characters' words or actions. For example, in *Much Ado About Nothing*, Don John's deception of Claudio into believing his fiancée Hero is unfaithful highlights the theme of appearance and reality.

Characters' speeches often highlight themes. In *Macbeth*, Lady Macbeth urges her husband to murder King Duncan. When Macbeth falters, she tells him: 'When you durst [dared to] do it, then you were a man.' She is saying that Macbeth is a coward. However, her words are linked to the theme of ambition, making us question who is the more ambitious of the two.

> **TOP TIP** ★
>
> You can split quotations, placing a word or words in one part of the sentence and the remaining words in another part, to make your writing more fluent.

❶ Write down the themes listed above that feature in the Shakespeare play you are studying. Add any others you can think of.

❷ Make notes on where the themes occur. Find quotations to support your points. Note them and keep them for reference.

❸ Choose a theme in the Shakespeare play you are studying and write a short commentary on it like the one in the Exam Focus section opposite.

THEMES IN NOVELS AND MODERN DRAMA

Themes in novels and drama can be revealed through almost all aspects of the text, including character, plot, **narrative voice**, **setting** and language. Here are some common themes with examples of how they can be revealed:

- **Theme:** Dual nature
  Example of how revealed: through character. In *The Strange Case of Dr Jekyll and Mr Hyde*, the writer explores the idea that humans are both good and evil. William Golding also explores this theme in *Lord of the Flies*, as does Dennis Kelly in his play *DNA*.

- **Theme:** Scientific knowledge and its dangers
  Example of how revealed: through plot. In *Frankenstein*, Victor attempts to create life. The terrifying consequences raise several moral issues. The modern novel *Never Let Me Go* explores related themes through human cloning.

- **Theme:** Marriage
  Example of how revealed: through narrative voice. In *Pride and Prejudice*, the opening sentence introduces the main theme – marriage.

EXAM FOCUS

Read this student's comment on *Romeo and Juliet*. Note how it breaks down the theme:

> Shakespeare shows how conflict can develop when, in Act I, Capulet appears to believe that Juliet is too young to marry since she is 'yet a stranger in the world'. However, by Act III he is less tolerant when she refuses to marry Paris, and determines to 'drag' her to church 'on a hurdle' if she disobeys him. His comments not only reveal his changed attitude but also highlight the position of women and the pressure on Elizabethan daughters to obey their fathers.

Shows how the relationship has altered

Identifies a related theme

Specific thematic comment linked to context

RECORDING EVIDENCE

In the exam you may be asked how themes are revealed in your text. You will need to make references and include short quotations.

❹ Decide which of the themes apply to your modern text.

> conflict   social class   money   love   friendship   loyalty   crime and punishment   prejudice
> childhood and growing up   ambition   the position of women   forgiveness   addiction
> justice   fear   pride   self-knowledge   parenthood   miserliness   poverty

APPLYING YOUR SKILLS

❺ Choose a theme from the list above that applies to a text you are studying.
Find examples of how the theme is revealed through either character, plot, narrative voice, setting or language. Write a 100-word commentary on how the theme is explored.

Remember:

- Look for evidence of themes in characters' words and action.
- Use quotations to support your points.

PROGRESS LOG [tick the correct box]   Needs more work ☐   Getting there ☐   Under control ☐

WRITING ABOUT STRUCTURE AND PLOT

A01 **A02**

STRUCTURE

The scheme below is a way of showing the structure of a story – how a plot develops. This can be applied to any prose or drama text you are studying.

Stage	What it means
Exposition	Setting presented. Main characters introduced. Plot begins with a problem or conflict or change in situation.
Rising action	Further characters may be introduced. Complications or obstacles arise related to the main conflict. Leads towards **climax**.
Climax	Defining moment of play or novel, on which future of main characters and events turn. Moment of greatest tension.
Falling action	Tension falls, although there may be moments of further tension/ uncertainty. Story moves towards ending.
Dénouement	Story's outcome, good or bad. Problems unravelled. Something usually learned. Characters have been affected.

This structure is represented visually in 'Freytag's Pyramid', created by the nineteenth-century novelist Gustav Freytag:

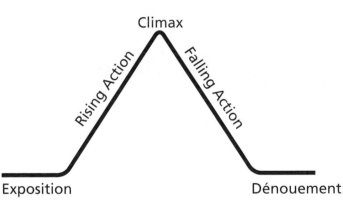

TOP TIP ⭐

In longer novels and plays, look out for a range of obstacles or reversals faced by the main character or characters. There will also be several moments of drama leading to a final, more important one.

❶ Make a two-column table for a text you are studying. Copy the stage from the table above in the left-hand column. In the right-hand column, make notes on how each stage could apply to your chosen text.

STRUCTURE IN SHAKESPEARE

Shakespeare's plays all have five acts, with a variable number of scenes within each act. Shakespeare often creates a **subplot** that reflects the main plot. For example, in *Much Ado About Nothing*, the subplot of Benedick and Beatrice being tricked into falling in love reflects, but also contrasts with, the main plot in which Claudio is tricked into rejecting Hero. Plays without a subplot, such as *Macbeth*, are often more intense.

GET IT RIGHT! ⭐

Never simply retell the story without offering any analysis. The examiner knows the story, and will see this as a sign of a weak candidate.

❷ Write down the main characters in the Shakespeare play you are studying, then note the plots that they are linked to.

STRUCTURE IN NOVELS AND MODERN DRAMA

A novel or play may:

- Use **flashbacks**, as in *Never Let Me Go*, in which most of the story is told in flashback by a first-person narrator. *A Christmas Carol* also uses **flash-forwards** to reveal a possible future
- Use **framing** (a story within a story), like *Frankenstein* or *The Curious Incident of the Dog in the Night-time* (a play within a play)
- Be in chronological order but use letters to move the plot along, as in *Pride and Prejudice*
- Be told chronologically, but present the main character's life from childhood (a **bildungsroman**), as in *Jane Eyre* and *Great Expectations* Alternatively, a text may focus on a shorter period as in *Anita and Me*, which describes two years in the narrator's childhood
- Use **foreshadowing** – hinting at what is to come, as in *Never Let Me Go*
- Have a separate narrator, as in the musical *Blood Brothers*, in which the narrator speaks directly to the audience

GET IT RIGHT!

Do not confuse form and structure. 'Form' is the particular type of text the writer chooses to tell their story – for example, short play, **novella**, **fable** (such as *Animal Farm*). Structure is the organisation and development of the plot within that form.

EXAM FOCUS

See how one student describes foreshadowing in *Lord of the Flies*:

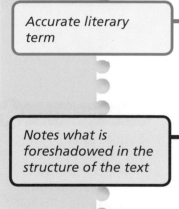

Accurate literary term

Notes what is foreshadowed in the structure of the text

Golding uses foreshadowing when Roger bullies the younger Henry. He throws stones towards him, but he leaves 'a space round' him so the stones miss, because despite his bullying, he still obeys some rules of civilised behaviour. This foreshadows the incident in Chapter 11. Roger rolls a boulder downhill and kills Piggy. Golding shows us at this point that all rules have now gone.

Example of foreshadowing

Effect on reader

APPLYING YOUR SKILLS

❸ Write 100 words on one aspect of the structure of a text you are studying.

Remember:

- Open with information about the basic structure of chapters or acts.
- Identify a structural feature, with an example, and explain its effects.

PROGRESS LOG [tick the correct box]　Needs more work ■　Getting there ■　Under control ■

COMMENTING ON KEY LITERARY TECHNIQUES   (A01) (A02)

Writers use many techniques to create effects. The most common is **imagery**, which includes **similes** and **metaphors**.

LITERARY TECHNIQUE: IMAGE

What is an image?	In literature, an image is the mental picture that appeals to the senses and is conjured up by the words.
Example	*'Tammy's sunburned skin was peeling off like the bark of a birch tree.'*
Effect	This simile visually describes the skin and is appropriate because the character is someone who spends a lot of time in nature.

LITERARY TECHNIQUE: METAPHOR

What is metaphor?	When a striking image is used to describe one thing as another to imply a resemblance.
Example	*'The Spider, as Mr Jaggers had called him [Bentley Drummle], was used to lying in wait.'* (Charles Dickens, *Great Expectations*)
Effect	The 'Spider' suggests someone who plots, waiting for the right moment to make a move or attack.

❶ In *Great Expectations*, Pip refers to another character, Joe, as a 'Hercules'. Write a sentence explaining the impression this metaphor creates. You may need to look up who Hercules was.

LITERARY TECHNIQUE: SYMBOLISM

What is symbolism?	When something such as an image, person or animal represents an abstract idea or quality that is widely understood.
Example	In *An Inspector Calls*, Eva Smith is a **symbol** of the poor and powerless.
Effect	It makes the idea real and vivid so that the audience is engaged with the issue. Here, the symbolism is used to question a society that allows the powerful to take no responsibility for the poor.

GET IT RIGHT! ⭐

Similes and metaphors both make comparisons between one thing and another. To tell the difference, remember that similes include the words 'like', 'as' or 'than' ('caught **like** a bird in a snare').

LITERARY TECHNIQUE: DRAMATIC IRONY

What is dramatic irony?	When the development of the plot allows the audience to know something that a character or characters do not.
Example	In *Blood Brothers*, Mickey and Edward meet and play together as children. They become blood brothers (cut their skin and mix their blood), which means they will always have to support each other.
Effect	The audience, which already knows the outcome, cannot but help feel sadness for the two small boys, because they are twins although they do not know it. Nor do they know that in the final act, Mickey will accidentally shoot Edward and will himself be shot by the police.

TOP TIP

Many of Shakespeare's plays contain dramatic irony. Note any examples of this technique in the play you are studying and make sure you understand why they are ironic.

Dramatic irony is a powerful technique. It often occurs in three stages:

- **Preparation:** The reader or audience or a particular character is made aware of something that the characters do not know.
- **Suspension:** The reader or audience becomes intrigued about what will happen; the character who has knowledge has to live with what he or she knows and decide whether to reveal it.
- **Resolution:** The truth is revealed, and the effect creates an outcome (which may or may not have been expected).

Dramatic irony can be used to tragic effect. In Shakespeare's *Romeo and Juliet*, Romeo thinks Juliet is dead and takes poison so he too will die. However, unlike Romeo, the audience – powerless to intervene – knows that Juliet is only in a deep sleep.

VOCABULARY CHOICES

Heightened language, such as powerful images, has a dramatic effect that grabs the reader's attention. Read this extract from *The Strange Case of Dr Jekyll and Mr Hyde*, in which vocabulary choices have specific effects:

Compound adjective and **abstract noun** evoke image of a creature out of control

And next moment, with ape-like fury *he was trampling his victim underfoot and* hailing down *a storm of blows, under which the bones were audibly shattered.*

Powerful verb conveys image of a violent onslaught

TOP TIP

When studying a text, compile a list of examples of literary techniques the writer uses to describe character, setting and key events. Note their effects and commit them to memory so you can recall them in the exam.

❷ Write a comment on the effect of the phrase 'the bones were audibly shattered'.

SENTENCE STRUCTURE

Writers also construct sentences to have particular effects on a reader. Look at the further example from *The Strange Case of Dr Jekyll and Mr Hyde* on the next page.

… yet, it was not so much these tokens of a swift physical decay that arrested the lawyer's notice, as a look in the eye and quality of manner that seemed to testify to some deep-seated terror of the mind.

Withholds most dramatic thought until the end to increase tension

The author might have written:

What arrested the lawyer's attention was the look in his eye and the quality of his manner that seemed to testify to some deep-seated terror of the mind, as well as the tokens of his swift physical decay.

Has less impact when placed in the middle (or beginning) of the sentence.

TOP TIP

When you read a text or extract, listen for the pace and **cadence** of sentences and paragraphs to see how the writer structures them for maximum effect.

APPLYING YOUR SKILLS

❸ Read this further extract from *The Strange Case of Dr Jekyll and Mr Hyde*, then answer the question below.

Sir, if that was my master, why had he a mask upon his face? If it was my master, why did he cry out like a rat and run from me? I have served him long enough. And then … the man paused and passed a hand over his face.

Think about techniques, sentences and vocabulary used for effect. Describe the effects of this extract in fifty words.

Remember:

* Sentence form has an effect.
* Similes are significant.
* Actions can reveal character.

PROGRESS CHECK FOR CHAPTER 7

GOOD PROGRESS

I can:

* Explain how writers use language to show action, ideas, character and mood ☐
* Use a selection of common literary terms to explain the effects of language ☐
* Refer to evidence, use appropriate quotations to support my points and make references to relevant parts of texts to show how a writer uses language ☐

EXCELLENT PROGRESS

I can:

* Analyse in detail and show how a writer uses language to explore characters and themes and create mood ☐
* Choose appropriate evidence, make inferences, include apt quotations and references and develop wider interpretations from a writer's use of language ☐
* Explain the function of settings and the effects of context ☐

CHAPTER 8: Paper 1, Sections A and B: Shakespeare and the nineteenth-century novel

WHAT'S IT ALL ABOUT?

In Paper 1 you will have to:

- Answer one question on the Shakespeare play you have studied (Section A)
- Answer one question on the nineteenth-century text you have studied (Section B)

In each case, you will need to write about the whole text, starting with an analysis of a short passage.

TIMING AND APPROACH

You will have one hour and forty-five minutes for the whole paper. You may find it useful to read through both questions for the two texts you have studied first (one in Section A and one in Section B), then return to Section A and read the extract and question more carefully. Annotate the extract and highlight the key words in the question to focus your mind. Then write your essay. When you have finished, do the same for Section B.

If you spend a total of fifteen minutes on reading, annotating and planning, and allow a total of ten minutes for checking, you will have forty minutes to write each essay. Bear in mind, however, that there are 4 marks for writing technique and accuracy for Section A (see below), so be extra careful when checking this.

> **TOP TIP** ⭐
>
> When writing about context, make sure it is really relevant to your analysis of the text, not just added on as an afterthought.

EARNING THE MARKS

There are 64 marks for the whole paper: 30 for each section, plus 4 for technique and accuracy in Section A. The table below shows how the marks are allocated.

PAPER 2, SECTIONS A AND B

Marks	What they are for	What this means
12	AO1	How well you understand and respond to the text; how you respond to the task – your essay-writing technique.
12	AO2	How effectively you analyse the author's language, form and structure, using subject terminology where appropriate.
6	AO3	Your understanding of context, including: how the text was influenced by the values of its time; its setting, social structures, etc.; its literary genre (e.g. tragedy or novella); and how different audiences might respond to it (e.g. modern compared with Shakespearean or nineteenth-century).
4	AO4 (Section A only)	Your use of vocabulary and sentence structures, and the accuracy of your spelling, grammar and punctuation.

WRITING ABOUT AN EXTRACT AND THEN THE WHOLE TEXT

There is no strict rule about how much time to spend analysing the extract and the whole text. However, you must tackle both to show you know the text well and can analyse the language in it.

A01

PAPER 1, SECTIONS A AND B

RESPONDING TO THE SHAKESPEARE EXTRACT

The question will provide an extract of 20–30 lines and remind you where it comes in the play. A *Much Ado About Nothing* question focusing on the section in which Beatrice tells Benedick to 'Kill Claudio', might be:

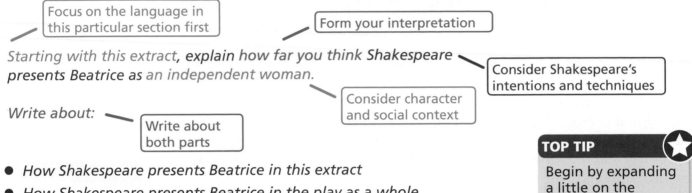

| Focus on the language in this particular section first |

| Form your interpretation |

Starting with this extract, **explain how far you think Shakespeare presents Beatrice as** *an independent woman.*

| Consider Shakespeare's intentions and techniques |

| Consider character and social context |

Write about:

| Write about both parts |

- *How Shakespeare presents Beatrice in this extract*
- *How Shakespeare presents Beatrice in the play as a whole*

The question will encourage a personal response. The two-part format is also an invitation to ask yourself:

- Is this extract typical of this character or **theme**, or are there contradictions to explore?
- Is there development or contrast even within the extract?

TOP TIP ★

Begin by expanding a little on the introduction provided in the exam paper, to make it clear that you know how the extract fits into the play.

EXAM FOCUS

Here is the start of a response to the *Much Ado About Nothing* question:

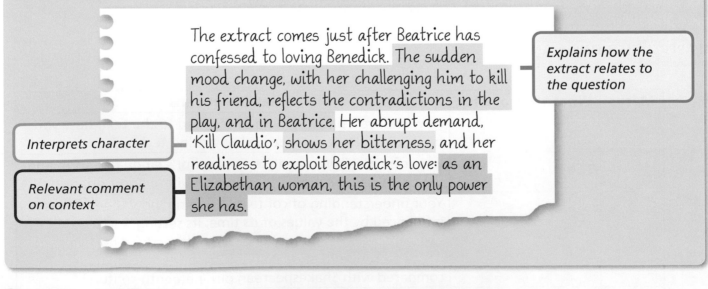

The extract comes just after Beatrice has confessed to loving Benedick. The sudden mood change, with her challenging him to kill his friend, reflects the contradictions in the play, and in Beatrice. Her abrupt demand, 'Kill Claudio', shows her bitterness, and her readiness to exploit Benedick's love: as an Elizabethan woman, this is the only power she has.

| Explains how the extract relates to the question |

| Interprets character |

| Relevant comment on context |

❶ Make up a similar question for the play you are studying. Focus on a short extract and one or more characters and write the question in the same format as the sample above. When you have decided on your question, write an opening to it.

RESPONDING TO THE NINETEENTH-CENTURY NOVEL EXTRACT

The format of the nineteenth-century novel question is the same as for the Shakespeare question. You will need to analyse the language, form and structure of the extract, and relate an aspect of the extract to the novel as a whole. You might be asked to write about one or more characters, or a theme.

You will need to:

● Focus on the aspect of the extract and novel highlighted in the question
● Show you understand the extract and the text as a whole
● Show you understand the significance of the extract for the question
● Analyse the writer's technique in the extract

Here is a typical question on the part of *Great Expectations* when Pip meets Miss Havisham, beginning *'She was dressed in rich materials ...'* (Chapter 8).

> *Starting with this extract, write about how Dickens represents the role of Miss Havisham in Pip's life.*
>
> *Write about:*
>
> ● *How Dickens represents Pip's response to Miss Havisham in this extract*
> ● *How Dickens represents Miss Havisham's influence on Pip in the novel as a whole*

The first bullet invites you to comment on:

● Miss Havisham (an embittered woman who has never recovered from being abandoned on her wedding day years earlier)
● Pip's apparent response to her as shown in his first-person narrative
● How Dickens presents both of these through his descriptions and language, together with the structure of the passage

In response to the second bullet, you would need to think about how Pip's life is changed by his relationship with Miss Havisham.

APPLYING YOUR SKILLS

❷ Choose a passage of 20–30 lines in the nineteenth-century novel you are studying and make up a question on it in the same format as the examples above.

❸ Write a response to the first part of the question, analysing the extract.

Remember:

● The question must deal with a specific extract and the text as a whole.
● Analyse the writer's techniques.

TRACING THEMES, VIEWPOINTS AND PERSPECTIVES

The question for your Shakespeare play or nineteenth-century novel may ask you to write about a **theme** or about 'attitudes':

- **Theme:** a big idea explored during the course of the text, such as ambition, power or love and marriage.
- **Attitudes:** how different characters, and the writer, seem to feel about something – for example, women, science, marriage or art.

Begin by examining how the theme or attitude is presented in the extract provided. Remember to comment on how it is reflected in the language. Then write about how this theme or viewpoint is explored in the whole text.

PAPER 1, SECTIONS A AND B

TOP TIP

You can refer back to the extract in your response even once you have started writing about the whole text. Your answer will be marked as a whole, not as two separate parts.

THEMES AND VIEWPOINTS IN SHAKESPEARE

Many themes appear in more than one of Shakespeare's plays:

- **Power and ambition:** Characters plot or plan to seize or retain power. This is often related to ideas about kingship and who is the 'rightful' ruler and ideas about conscience, guilt and good/evil.
- **Fate, destiny:** This is the idea that a particular outcome is inevitable; characters may seem doomed. This may be contrasted with the view that human beings have free will.
- **Love and marriage:** Characters fall in love, perhaps with unsuitable people; their love may be tested; they may want to marry against a parent's wishes; they may even die for love.
- **Appearance and reality:** It may be unclear what is real (for example, if a character sees a ghost); some characters may lie or disguise themselves.
- **Loyalty and betrayal:** Loyalty to a king or lord was greatly respected in Shakespeare's time. Characters may experience divided loyalties.
- **Revenge and justice:** Characters may seek revenge and die achieving it. They may struggle to be treated fairly, or to ensure that someone else is.
- **Child-parent conflict:** Parents may want to control adult children (for example, who they marry).

❶ Find a section of the play you are studying that reflects one of these themes. Think of three other examples of the theme elsewhere in the play. Look them up and write down suitable short quotations that you could comment on.

GET IT RIGHT!

Be sure to discuss more than one example of the theme or viewpoint.

THEMES AND ATTITUDES IN THE NINETEENTH-CENTURY NOVEL

Themes and attitudes vary more across the range of nineteenth-century novels. However, some broad themes occur frequently:

- Love and marriage (*Pride and Prejudice, Jane Eyre*)
- Conflict (*The Strange Case of Doctor Jekyll and Mr Hyde*)
- Family (*Great Expectations, A Christmas Carol*)
- Individuals and society (*Jane Eyre, A Christmas Carol*)

- Pride (*Frankenstein, Pride and Prejudice*)
- Justice (*The Sign of the Four, Frankenstein*)

Some questions on themes may be set in terms of 'attitudes'. For example, for *Frankenstein* you might be given a section including the following extract:

> *One man's life or death were but a small price to pay for the acquirement of the knowledge which I sought; for the dominion I should acquire and transmit over the elemental foes of our race.*
>
> (Walton, Letter IV)

A question on this might be:

> *Starting with this extract, how does the writer present attitudes towards science?*

EXAM FOCUS ✎

Here is part of a response to the question about *Frankenstein*. Note how it moves from the extract to the novel as a whole:

> Walton shows here that his motivation for discovery is personal glory. He is prepared to sacrifice 'every hope' for the power brought by knowledge. His use of the abstract noun 'dominion' suggests his grand view of the power he will hold. Shelley's attitude to science, however, is not merely negative. Frankenstein's Creature is at first noble and sensitive, as shown by his love of poetry.

Makes a point based on the extract

Analyses language using an appropriate term

Topic sentence announces first example of a different view

APPLYING YOUR SKILLS ✓

❷ Find a passage focusing on a theme in the novel you are studying – perhaps using the list opposite. Make notes on how your chosen passage explores this theme.

❸ Write part of a response to a question on your passage and theme, in which you shift from the extract to the novel as a whole.

Remember:

- Link the extract to the novel as a whole.
- The author may use a character to explore a theme.
- Language choices may reflect a theme.

TACKLING SHAKESPEARE'S LANGUAGE

Shakespeare was writing over 400 years ago so the language he uses might seem difficult to understand today. This unit is designed to help you to understand and appreciate Shakespeare's language.

PAPER 1, SECTION A

READING BLANK VERSE

Shakespeare sometimes uses **prose**, especially for lower-class characters, but large sections of his plays are written in **blank verse** – poetry that is unrhymed ('blank') – and in a **metre** called **iambic pentameter**. In this form, each line has five (*pent*) iams. An iam is a pair of syllables, one unstressed, one stressed.

Read the line below out loud, stressing the underlined syllables:

> O, <u>par</u>don <u>me</u>, thou <u>bleed</u>ing <u>piece</u> of <u>earth</u>

Sometimes Shakespeare varies this:

- To emphasise meaning
- To convey a speaker's emotions
- To make the speech sound more natural

Read these lines from *Macbeth* aloud:

> *Tomorrow, and tomorrow, and tomorrow,*
> *Creeps in this petty pace from day to day*
> *To the last syllable of recorded time.*

None of these lines is quite iambic pentameter. Why? At this point, Macbeth is losing a battle and has just heard of his wife's suicide. The rhythm shows his feeling that life drags on pointlessly. The first line is not iambic at all, and it has an extra syllable. This makes it drag. To make sense of the second line, you have to stress the first word, emphasising the slowness of time. The third line also varies rhythm and has an extra, dragging syllable.

❶ Read a verse speech from the play you are studying.
- Read to the ends of sentences, not to the ends of lines.
- Tap out the lines to check their rhythm.
- If a line varies from iambic pentameter, try to work out how the sense is affected.

TOP TIP ⭐

Tap out the rhythm of a line from the Shakespeare play you are studying to see if it is in exact iambic pentameter. If it varies, try to work out why.

GET IT RIGHT! ⭐

The lines from *Macbeth* show another important point: you should read Shakespeare following the punctuation; you should not read each line separately.

TOP TIP ⭐

Shakespeare sometimes uses **rhyming couplets** (pairs of rhyming lines). Romeo's speech in this example is all in rhyming couplets. This suggests the romantic nature of the speech. Rhyming couplets can also be used at the end of a speech or scene, giving a sense of completion.

THE ROLE OF IMAGERY

Shakespeare uses **imagery** to express meaning and reflect the **themes** of the plays. This imagery might be:

- **Metaphor:** *'he sees the Romans are but sheep'* (Cassius, *Julius Caesar*)
- **Simile:** *'As two spent swimmers, that do cling together / And choke their art'* (Sergeant describing warring sides in an indecisive battle, *Macbeth*)
- **Personification:** *'when you depart from me, sorrow abides and happiness takes his leave'* (Leonato addressing Don Pedro in *Much Ado About Nothing*)

Some plays use a great deal of particular types of imagery. For example, *Macbeth* and *Julius Caesar* have many examples of animal imagery, emphasising the predatory animal aspect of human nature.

❷ Read these lines from *Romeo and Juliet*. Romeo has just seen Juliet for the first time:

It seems she hangs upon the cheek of night
Like a rich jewel in an Ethiope's[1] ear;
Beauty too rich for use, for earth too dear.

Ethiope[1] – Ethiopian (someone who has dark skin)

- How do these lines use all three types of image?
- How do these images suggest what Romeo feels about Juliet?
- How might Romeo's plentiful use of imagery reflect his character?

EXAM FOCUS

Read this extract from a student's essay discussing imagery in *Much Ado About Nothing*. Some of its features have been highlighted:

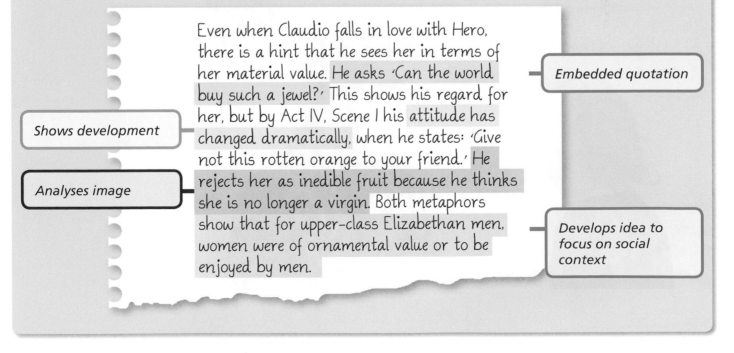

Even when Claudio falls in love with Hero, there is a hint that he sees her in terms of her material value. He asks 'Can the world buy such a jewel?' This shows his regard for her, but by Act IV, Scene I his attitude has changed dramatically, when he states: 'Give not this rotten orange to your friend.' He rejects her as inedible fruit because he thinks she is no longer a virgin. Both metaphors show that for upper-class Elizabethan men, women were of ornamental value or to be enjoyed by men.

Embedded quotation

Shows development

Analyses image

Develops idea to focus on social context

APPLYING YOUR SKILLS

❸ Find a speech in the play you are studying that contains imagery. Write a paragraph about it like the one in the Exam Focus response, but include a comment on the rhythm of the language used in the speech.

Remember:

● Identify the type of image.

● Quote it.

● Analyse its effect.

● Develop by explaining how it relates to a character, theme, or both in the play.

PROGRESS CHECK FOR CHAPTER 8

GOOD PROGRESS

I can:

● Relate an extract to a whole text ☐

● Identify and write about themes and attitudes ☐

● Broadly understand Shakespeare's language ☐

EXCELLENT PROGRESS

I can:

● Analyse the language of an extract and a whole text in detail ☐

● Explore themes and attitudes as expressed by characters and in language ☐

● Analyse the effects of Shakespeare's language ☐

CHAPTER 9: Paper 2, Section A: Modern prose and drama

WHAT'S IT ALL ABOUT?

In Paper 2, Section A of your Literature exam, you will answer one question out of a choice of two on your modern set text. The first option is likely to be character-based and the second theme-based. The first option may ask how the writer uses a particular character to explore ideas about a given **theme**.

TIMING AND APPROACH

You will have two hours and fifteen minutes for the whole of Paper 2, which is in three sections. Each section carries about a third of the marks, so you should aim to spend about forty-five minutes on Section A, including planning and checking.

EARNING THE MARKS

There are 96 marks for the whole of Paper 2. Section A carries 30 marks for content and an extra 4 marks for technique and accuracy. The table below shows how the marks are allocated for Section A:

PAPER 2, SECTION A

Marks	What they are for	What this means
12	AO1	How well you understand and respond to the text and task; including your essay-writing techniques, such as the use of textual evidence, especially quotations.
12	AO2	Your ability to analyse the author's use of language, form and structure, using subject terminology where appropriate
6	AO3	Your understanding of context, including: how the text was influenced by the values of its time; its setting, social structures, etc.
4	AO4 (Section A only)	Your use of vocabulary, sentence structures, and the accuracy of your spelling, grammar and punctuation.

GET IT RIGHT!

Answer exactly the question given. For example, if asked how a character relates to a theme, do not simply write everything you know about the character or the theme.

TOP TIP

The question will give you two bullet point prompts to tell you what to write about. These may simply break down the main question, but they may also give you a little more information.

TYPES OF QUESTION AND HOW TO RESPOND TO THEM

The question is not designed to trick you, but you should read it carefully to make sure you understand exactly what you need to do.

A01

PAPER 1, SECTION A

DECODING A CHARACTER-BASED QUESTION

A typical character question might be:

> Invites you to make a judgement about how much this is true

> Focuses on Golding's techniques

> Points towards a particular view you must consider

*How far **does Golding present** Simon as a victim in Lord of the Flies?*

Write about:

> Reminds you to analyse Golding's techniques

- *How Golding presents **the character of Simon***
- *How far you sympathise with Simon*

> Links to 'victim', inviting your response

How would you answer this question? Consider:

- Whether Simon is a victim, and if so, in what way (for example, being mocked by other boys)
- How Golding describes Simon as sensitive and insightful (for example, his understanding of what is going wrong on the island, particularly descriptions of his behaviour and appearance)
- The way in which he is mistaken for 'the Beast' and killed
- Your personal response, assessing 'how far you sympathise'

A slightly different type of question might highlight one role played by a character:

> *How does Priestley present Arthur Birling as a parent in An Inspector Calls?*
>
> *Write about:*
>
> - *How Priestley presents the character of Arthur Birling*
> - *How Priestley uses Birling to explore ideas about fatherhood*

1 Here is another type of question, linking character to **theme**. Even if you are not studying the novel, try to decode the question, identifying the key words and what they are asking you to do.

> *How does Golding use Piggy to explore ideas about civilisation in* Lord of the Flies?
>
> *Write about:*
>
> - *How Golding presents the character of Piggy*
> - *How Golding uses Piggy to explore ideas about civilisation*

TOP TIP ★

If you are asked to write about one aspect of a character, do not discuss other aspects. However, there may be room for interpretation – for example, you could link Birling's harsh parenting to his attitude as an employer.

DECODING A THEME-BASED QUESTION

A typical theme question might be:

> *How does Priestley explore ideas about guilt and blame in* An Inspector Calls*?*
>
> *Write about:*
>
> - *Ideas about guilt and blame in* An Inspector Calls
> - *How Priestley presents these ideas through the way he writes*

How would you tackle this question if *An Inspector Calls* was your set text? You might consider:

- Whether there is a distinction between 'guilt' and 'blame' in the play – some characters feel guilty, others do not, but all blame someone
- Whether Priestley leaves the audience to reach a conclusion or conveys a particular message
- The dramatic techniques that Priestley uses, such as having a mysterious inspector appear who seems to know a great deal about each character
- The language used by characters
- The historical context of the play (written just after the Second World War)

TOP TIP

In every paragraph you write, check that you are still answering the question. If you find that you have strayed from the point, try to find a way of making your comments relevant.

EXAM FOCUS

Read this part of a successful response to the question about *An Inspector Calls*. Some of its features have been highlighted:

> Birling remembers Eva Smith as one of his employees, but, though he realises he might be blamed for her death, he insists, 'I can't accept any responsibility.' Sheila, on the other hand, becomes 'distressed' when hearing about the girl, and quickly regrets using her power as a wealthy customer to get her fired. Eric reacts even more strongly ...

Linking phrase to compare characters

Knowledgeable reference to text as evidence of guilt

Effective use of embedded quotation relating to 'guilt and blame'

APPLYING YOUR SKILLS

❷ Make a five- or six-bullet point plan for answering this exam-style question:

Write about the extent to which one of the main characters in your text changes or develops as the text progresses.

Write about:

- *What they are like at the start and end of the text*
- *How the writer presents the changes they undergo*

PROGRESS LOG [tick the correct box]   Needs more work ■   Getting there ■   Under control ■

TRACING THEMES AND CHARACTERS ACROSS A TEXT

The texts you will be studying are largely 'character-driven', which means that the plot gradually emerges from the characters. Characters change over the course of the story – for example, learning from mistakes. You may have to write about this in your exam.

A01

PAPER 2, SECTION A

TRACING CHARACTER DEVELOPMENT

When answering questions about character development, you will need to select key moments in the text – rather like points on a graph – and see how the character is presented at each point. Think about:

- What they do – for example, how they treat other characters
- What they say and how this reveals what they are like
- How others respond to or behave towards them

A typical question of this type might be:

| Two aspects – ways she changes and reasons for these changes | Focus on one character – Meena |

How and why does Meena change in Anita and Me?

Write about:

| Implies character growth and that there is more than one way |

- *The ways Meena develops over the course of the novel*
- *How Syal presents Meena's development*

| Syal's writing techniques |

RESPONDING EFFECTIVELY

A good response to this question might focus on:

- What Meena is like at the start of the novel, perhaps showing how Syal portrays her through the first-person narrative
- Three or four key incidents that change her, and how they are presented or described by the writer
- Other characters, tied in to these incidents, who change her – Anita, Nanima, Sam
- What Meena is like at the end of the novel

❶ Make brief notes on how one character develops in a modern text you are studying.

TOP TIP ⭐

If you are asked how a writer explores a theme, think about which characters relate to that theme, and how they are used to explore it. Then make brief notes on key moments when something they do or say contributes to the development of the theme.

EXAM FOCUS

Read the start of a response to the question about *Anita and Me*. Some of its features have been highlighted:

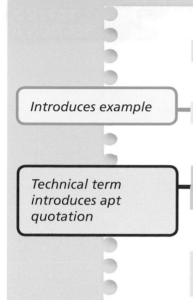

At the start of the novel, Meena is nine. Syal's first-person narrative combines childish attitudes with the insights of the adult Meena reflecting on her childhood. So, for example, she portrays herself as being addicted to drama and exaggeration. There is adult irony in her rhetorical question 'When would anything dangerous and cruel ever happen to me?' The novel could be seen as the story of her getting what she longs for. Several 'dangerous and cruel' things happen to her, so that she grows up considerably in two years.

Introduces example

Technical term introduces apt quotation

Starts to address author's techniques

Maintains focus on 'change'; prepares reader for the rest of the response

What mistakes **might** a student have made when answering this question?

- They might simply retell the story without analysing what happens.
- They might explain **how** Meena changes, but not **why**.
- They might look at isolated incidents without giving an overview of character development.
- They might describe other characters without focusing on their influence on Meena.
- They might forget to write about techniques, such as the first-person narrative.

TOP TIP

If you cannot quote exactly, it is acceptable to write, for example, 'Meena admits that she considers lying to the police.'

HOW THEMES DEVELOP

Themes may also be developed or explored through characters. One example in *Anita and Me* is the theme of friendship. The narrator, Meena, has a friend, Anita, whom she admires but who is selfish and a bad influence. Meena comes to recognise Anita's faults and value other more supportive characters. The character and the theme develop side by side.

APPLYING YOUR SKILLS

❷ Choose a theme in a text you are studying and note down three moments when it is developed somehow in the text.

PROGRESS LOG [tick the correct box]   Needs more work ◻   Getting there ◻   Under control ◻

TACKLING MODERN DRAMA STRUCTURES

Commenting on structure involves 'taking a step back' from the text and considering the overall development of the story. Structure is especially important in plays, because unlike other literary forms, plays are designed to be performed to an audience that will experience it all in one sitting. A performance has an emotional effect, leading to **catharsis**: the release of emotional tension.

PAPER 2, SECTION A

THE FIVE-POINT STORY DESIGN

Plays are often described as hanging on five points:

- **The inciting incident:** This is the key event that triggers the main action. It could be in the opening scene, or it may have already happened and be reported (as in *An Inspector Calls*).

- **Successes and reverses:** These are ups and downs in the main characters' lives as they struggle to achieve their goals. In *An Inspector Calls*, this particularly relates to Eva Smith, who is already dead at the start of the play. Her successes and reverses are tied up with the Birling family, each of whom discovers their effect on her.

- **Crisis:** This is the point when there is most at stake for the characters – when it appears they could win or lose, survive or collapse. In *Blood Brothers*, this is when Mickey hears that his 'blood brother' Edward is having an affair with his wife Linda, and he goes to confront Edward with a gun.

- **Climax:** This is the point of greatest emotional tension, often coming straight after the crisis. In *An Inspector Calls*, this is arguably when the Inspector finally accuses the family, before walking out.

- **Resolution:** This is the point near the end when the tension of uncertainty is released. This conclusion could be tragic, as with the deaths at the end of *Blood Brothers*, or it could involve a reconciliation between characters, as between Jo and her mother Helen in *A Taste of Honey*.

However, bear in mind that audiences and readers may disagree where and when these five points occur, so make sure you have a good reason to interpret your play this way.

TOP TIP

The five-point story design also works for novels. Plays generally span a shorter period of time and feature fewer successes and reverses.

❶ Make a note of the five points and relate each one to a point or points in the drama you are studying.

EXAM FOCUS

Read this extract from a successful response to the question 'How does Priestley explore the theme of guilt and responsibility in *An Inspector Calls*?' Some of its features have been highlighted:

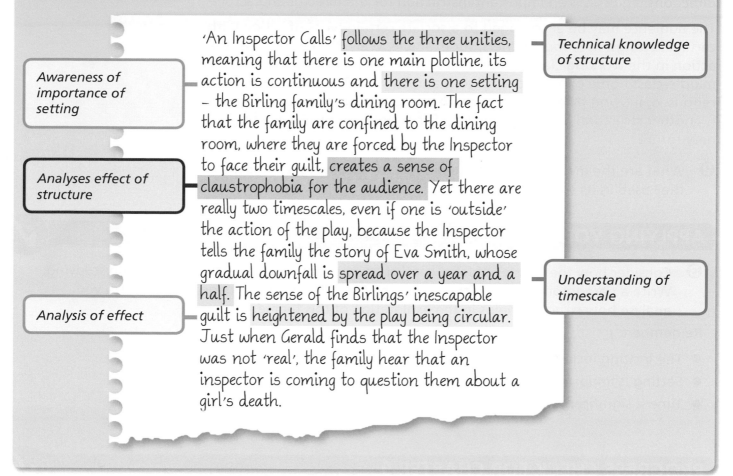

Awareness of importance of setting

Analyses effect of structure

Analysis of effect

'An Inspector Calls' follows the three unities, meaning that there is one main plotline, its action is continuous and there is one setting – the Birling family's dining room. The fact that the family are confined to the dining room, where they are forced by the Inspector to face their guilt, creates a sense of claustrophobia for the audience. Yet there are really two timescales, even if one is 'outside' the action of the play, because the Inspector tells the family the story of Eva Smith, whose gradual downfall is spread over a year and a half. The sense of the Birlings' inescapable guilt is heightened by the play being circular. Just when Gerald finds that the Inspector was not 'real', the family hear that an inspector is coming to question them about a girl's death.

Technical knowledge of structure

Understanding of timescale

What mistakes **might** a student have made in writing about structure in this response?

- They might have retold the story from beginning to end.
- They might have failed to take into account the narrated story of Eva Smith.
- They might have failed to comment on the effects of structure on the audience.
- They might have failed to analyse how structure develops the theme of guilt.

THE IMPORTANCE OF SETTING

The importance of setting in structure can be seen in the example of *An Inspector Calls*. A playwright will indicate where a scene is set in the **stage directions**, and this is an important instruction for the director and actors.

The audience may be encouraged to associate certain types of action with certain settings. In *Blood Brothers*, for example, Willy Russell contrasts the action in the working-class home of Mrs Johnstone and Mickey, and the middle-class home of Mr and Mrs Lyons and Edward. The Johnstones being rehoused, moving from the inner city to the country, at the start of Act 2, is another structural device: it seems as if they are going to have a bright new future.

❷   What are the main settings of the play you are studying, and how are they used in its structure?

APPLYING YOUR SKILLS

❸   Consider how the themes of love, conflict or inequality appear in the play you are studying. Write a paragraph, based on the one in the Exam Focus box on page 115, in which you analyse how structure helps in the exploration of this theme.

Remember:

● The inciting incident triggers the action.

● Setting is important in structure.

● Time is significant.

PROGRESS CHECK FOR CHAPTER 9

GOOD PROGRESS

I can:

● Decode a question on character or a theme ☐

● Trace character or theme development over a text ☐

● Identify the structure of a text ☐

EXCELLENT PROGRESS

I can:

● Understand the demands of different types of question ☐

● Write about how character development relates to the exploration of themes ☐

● Analyse a text in terms of the five-point story design and its setting ☐

CHAPTER 10: Paper 2, Section B: Poetry from the AQA Anthology

WHAT'S IT ALL ABOUT?

In Paper 2, Section B, you will have to answer the question given on whichever cluster of poems you have studied: 'Love and relationships' or 'Power and conflict'.

The question will ask you to **compare** how poets **present** attitudes to a particular **subject**, or ideas about a particular **theme**, in one specific poem and another poem of your choice from the cluster.

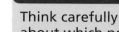
TOP TIP

Think carefully about which poems in the cluster would work best in comparison with the printed poem in terms of subject or theme. Then choose one that you know well.

TIMING AND APPROACH

You have two hours and fifteen minutes for the whole of Paper 2, which is in three sections. Each section carries about a third of the marks, so aim to spend about forty-five minutes on Section B, including planning and checking.

EARNING THE MARKS

There are 30 marks for Section B. The table below shows how they are allocated.

PAPER 2, SECTION B

Marks	What they are for	What this means
12	AO1	How well you understand and respond to the poems; how you respond to the task – your comparison techniques, including use of textual evidence, especially quotations.
12	AO2	How efficiently you analyse the poems' language, form and structure, using subject terminology where appropriate.
6	AO3	Your understanding of the relationship between the poems, and their contexts, including how they are influenced by the values of their time, etc.

TOP TIP

Stick to the focus of the question – for example, 'attitudes to parenting'. Do not just write a broad comparison of everything in both poems.

KEY POETIC TECHNIQUES

Commenting on 'how poets present' means analysing the techniques they use. You should analyse:

PAPER 2,
SECTION B

- Which techniques your two poems have in common
- How each poet uses these techniques
- How the poems differ (for example, one poem may use a single **metaphor**, while the other may use several **similes**)

METRE, RHYTHM AND RHYME

Like music, all poems have rhythm. This is created by the mixture of stressed and unstressed syllables when you speak a line aloud in a natural way. If this rhythm is used in a regular form, in lines of a particular length, and perhaps with the addition of rhyme, this creates a **metre**. Older poems are more likely to use a metre; modern poems are often freer in style, though they will still have rhythm.

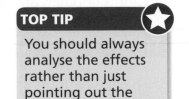

TOP TIP

You should always analyse the effects rather than just pointing out the techniques.

Look at this extract from Tennyson's 'The Charge of the Light Brigade'. The underlining shows the naturally stressed syllables:

> _<u>Half</u> a league, <u>half</u> a league[1],_
> _<u>Half</u> a league <u>on</u>ward,_
> _<u>All</u> in the <u>val</u>ley of <u>Death</u>_
> _<u>Rode</u> the six <u>hun</u>dred._
>
> _league[1] – about 600 miles_

The poem describes a cavalry charge of 600 men that took place in 1854. Read the lines aloud. Notice how the rhythm suggests steadily moving horses, especially in the first two lines. In addition, the 'd' sounds of 'Death / Rode ... hundred' could suggest the drumming of hooves.

This rhythm is unusual: a stressed syllable followed by two unstressed ones. It creates a sense of the men on their horses driving forward towards danger. This sense is strengthened by the repetition and the half-rhyme of 'onward' and 'hundred'.

1 Read the following lines aloud. Then copy the extract and work out where the stresses come. How are the rhythm and its effects different from Tennyson's poem?

> _She put my arm about her waist,_
> _And made her smooth white shoulder bare,_
> _And all her yellow hair displaced,_
> _And, stooping, made my cheek lie there._
>
> _'Porphyria's Lover' by Robert Browning_

EXAM FOCUS

Read this part of an analysis of Browning's poem. Some of its features are highlighted:

> Identifies poetic features, using correct terms

The regular iambic rhythm, lines of equal syllable-length, and regularly rhyming line-ends all help to create a sense of steady calm. The repetition of 'And' makes the lines almost hypnotic. The only slight pause draws our attention to the verb 'stooping', which suggests that Porphyria is symbolically lowering herself socially in visiting her lower-status lover, as well as physically stooping.

> Analyses effect

> Interprets symbolism

IMAGERY

Imagery is an important technique. Not all poems use it, but **metaphors**, **similes** or **personification** are often used to bring a description or idea to life.

In 'The Farmer's Bride', quoted below, the narrator is a farmer:

> Shy as a leveret,[1] swift as he,
> Straight and slight as a young larch tree,
> Sweet as the first wild violets, she,
> To her wild self. But what to me?
>
> leveret[1] – young hare

> **TOP TIP**
>
> Try to use correct literary terms, but embed them in your sentences. For example: 'The extended simile creates a sense of ...'.

❷ How do the similes the poet uses for the farmer's bride reflect his world, as well as creating a picture of the bride?

APPLYING YOUR SKILLS

In Thomas Hardy's 'Neutral Tones', the speaker bitterly recalls a meeting with a former lover:

> Your eyes on me were as eyes that rove
> Over tedious riddles of years ago;
> And some words played between us to and fro
> On which lost the more by our love.

❸ Write an analysis of the effects of the one image used here.

❹ Write another two or three sentences analysing the effects of rhythm and rhyme. Why do you think Hardy uses a half-rhyme (not a 'perfect rhyme') for lines 1 and 4?

PROGRESS LOG [tick the correct box]   Needs more work ■   Getting there ■   Under control ■

COMPARING POEMS

CHOOSING A SECOND POEM

A01 **A02** **A03**

PAPER 2,
SECTION B

In Section B, you must choose a poem to compare with the one given in the question. The paper will only give you the set poem in full, together with the titles of the other poems in the cluster, so you should choose a poem you can write about in detail from memory.

You should also take the wording of the question into account. For example:

> *Compare how poets present attitudes to love in 'Love's Philosophy' and* **one** *other poem from 'Love and relationships'.*

In theory, you could compare any two poems. However, you may find it easier to compare poems that have similar themes so that the differences in style are highlighted. For example, you could compare 'Love's Philosophy' with another poem about romantic love, rather than one about a family relationship such as 'Climbing My Grandfather' or 'Walking Away'.

APPROACHES TO COMPARISON

First, quickly annotate the set poem to remind yourself of its key themes and stylistic techniques. You could also write brief notes comparing the poem with the one you have chosen for the comparison.

Possible points to compare include:

- Subject and themes: do both poems present the same attitude to love? If not, in what ways are they different?
- Verse form (for example, **sonnet**)
- **Imagery – metaphor, simile, personification**
- Word choices – their meaning, tone and sound
- Viewpoint and voice (for example, first person addressing lover)
- Structure, including development and conclusion

The table below shows some points to compare for **subject** and **themes**, and **verse form**, in 'Love's Philosophy' and 'I think of thee!'

TOP TIP

Look for similarities between the poems as well as differences.

'Love's Philosophy'	'I think of thee!'
Shelley addresses the woman he loves, trying to persuade her to kiss him.	Browning addresses an established lover (her husband), describing her loving thoughts. She just wants to experience his presence, not be distracted by her own thoughts about him.
Regular rhyme and rhythm create a sense of harmony.	Sonnet form – traditional for love poetry.

You could then go on to compare imagery and ideas, as shown in the table below.

'Love's Philosophy'	'I think of thee!'
The poet uses natural phenomena (fountains, oceans, rivers, winds, etc.), with some personification, to persuade the woman to kiss him. His arguments are more playful than logical. The images move loosely from earth in **stanza** 1, to heaven, sun and moon in stanza 2.	The nature imagery creates a sense of growth in the relationship. The poet uses a single **extended metaphor** to explore the idea of her thoughts being like ivy on a tree (her husband).
The poet says nothing about the woman herself: he focuses on nature to make it sound completely natural for her to kiss him.	She portrays her lover as powerful: he has only to 'rustle' his 'boughs' to 'burst' through the ivy.

❶ Make a table of points for comparison.

- If you are studying the 'Love and relationships' cluster, compare 'Eden Rock' and one other poem in the cluster.

- If you are studying the 'Power and conflict' cluster, compare 'War Photographer' and one other poem.

EXAM FOCUS

Read this part of a comparison between 'Love's Philosophy' and 'I think of thee!', focusing on structure. Some of its features have been highlighted:

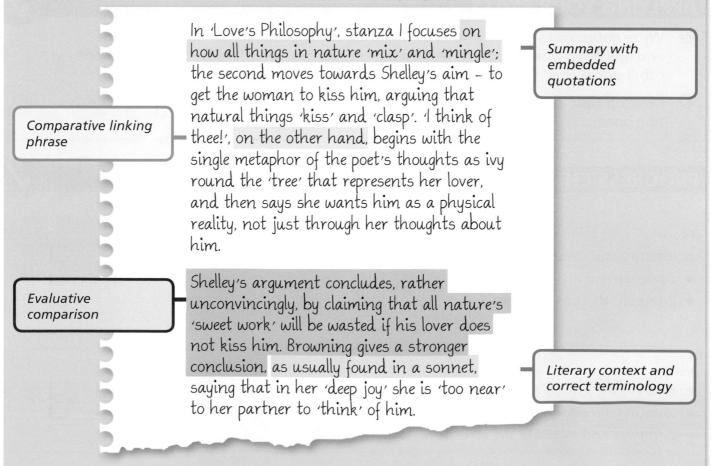

Comparative linking phrase

In 'Love's Philosophy', stanza I focuses on how all things in nature 'mix' and 'mingle'; the second moves towards Shelley's aim – to get the woman to kiss him, arguing that natural things 'kiss' and 'clasp'. 'I think of thee!', on the other hand, begins with the single metaphor of the poet's thoughts as ivy round the 'tree' that represents her lover, and then says she wants him as a physical reality, not just through her thoughts about him.

Summary with embedded quotations

Evaluative comparison

Shelley's argument concludes, rather unconvincingly, by claiming that all nature's 'sweet work' will be wasted if his lover does not kiss him. Browning gives a stronger conclusion, as usually found in a sonnet, saying that in her 'deep joy' she is 'too near' to her partner to 'think' of him.

Literary context and correct terminology

What mistakes **might** a candidate have made in answering this question?

● They might have just summarised the poems without really comparing them.

● They might have not analysed poetic techniques or language.

● They might have not used quotations as evidence.

● They might have not used, or incorrectly used, terminology.

APPLYING YOUR SKILLS ✔

❷ Write notes analysing the effects of two or three images in **either** 'Bayonet Charge' and one other poem from the 'Power and conflict' cluster **or** 'Walking Away' and one other poem from the 'Love and relationships' cluster.

❸ Develop your image analyses into one or two paragraphs comparing imagery in the two poems.

PROGRESS CHECK FOR CHAPTER 10 ✔

GOOD PROGRESS

I can:

● Identify and comment on metre, rhythm and rhyme ☐

● Comment on imagery ☐

● Compare themes in poems ☐

EXCELLENT PROGRESS

I can:

● Analyse the effects of variations in metre ☐

● Identify and closely analyse the effects of different types of imagery ☐

● Compare and evaluate the stylistic features of poems ☐

CHAPTER 11: Paper 2, Section C: Unseen poetry

WHAT'S IT ALL ABOUT?

In the Paper 2, Section C of your English Literature exam you will have to answer two questions:

- Question 1 will ask you to analyse an **unseen poem**, which will be given in full in the paper. The question may focus on how the poet presents feelings about something in the poem.

- Question 2 will provide you with the text of a **second poem** that is similar to the first in some ways. It will ask you to compare an aspect of both poems, such as how they present feelings about a child or a parent.

The wording of both questions may take the form: 'How does the poet present ...?' This means you must analyse how their style conveys their feelings or attitudes.

TOP TIP

There are no marks for spelling, punctuation or grammar in Paper 2, Section C. However, if you express yourself clearly and accurately it will be easier for the examiner to understand your answers and credit you for them.

TIMING AND APPROACH

You should spend about forty-five minutes on Section C, including about five minutes for planning. It is also important to allow five minutes at the end to check and improve your work.

EARNING THE MARKS

There are 96 marks for the whole of Paper 2, and 32 of these are for Section C. The table below shows how the Section C marks are allocated.

PAPER 2, SECTION C

Question	AO	Marks
1	AO1	12
	AO2	12
2	AO2	8

TACKLING AN UNSEEN POEM

You will be given poems you have not studied before (unseen poems) printed on the exam papers. The questions will focus on how the poet presents certain feelings or ideas. The stages below explain how to approach these questions.

STAGE 1: READ THE POEM AND THE QUESTION

- First read the poem through and try to understand what it is broadly about (such as conflict, relationships or a poem related to time and place).
- Read the poem again, keeping the exam question in mind.
- Reread any part of the poem (for example, a particular phrase, line or verse) if you are uncertain about its meaning. Try to understand it in relation to what the poem is broadly about.

STAGE 2: MAKE NOTES AND ANNOTATIONS ON THE PAGE

- Underline key words, **phrases** or lines in the poem.
- Identify the main **theme** or themes.
- Underline any images or techniques that might help you answer the question.
- Note any special features (such as layout or repeating patterns, such as recurring words or sounds) that enhance the meaning in relation to the question.
- Note what form (type of poem) it is where possible (such as **sonnet**, free verse) and whether this aids understanding (is there a change in **tone** or perspective after the first eight lines, as in a sonnet?)
- Note down some short questions or notes to help you. For example: *'alliteration stresses the stormy sea?'* or *'Image of a lost love, means honesty is important.'*

STAGE 3: WRITE YOUR RESPONSE

Organise your answer into six or seven paragraphs, referring to the main points from your annotations.

- Discuss (briefly) what happens in the poem; the 'story' and the context (setting, location, etc.) (Introduction).
- Explain what the speaker's feelings are in relation to the focus/theme of the question.
- Discuss images in the poem that portray the theme.
- Describe the techniques the poet uses to enhance the theme.
- Discuss the form and structure of the poem, and the effect each of these has on the reader.
- Sum up (concisely) what ideas the poet presents to the reader. (Conclusion)

For example, you might be asked:

> *How does the poet present the speaker's feelings about love and marriage in the poem?*

This suggests you should be looking for:

- What **sort of 'story'** the poet tells about love and marriage.
- The **viewpoint** or **emotions** that suggest an attitude to love and marriage
- Positive or negative language or descriptions
- The effect of the poet's choices

Study the poem 'Postponement' below, and the annotations written in response to the question:

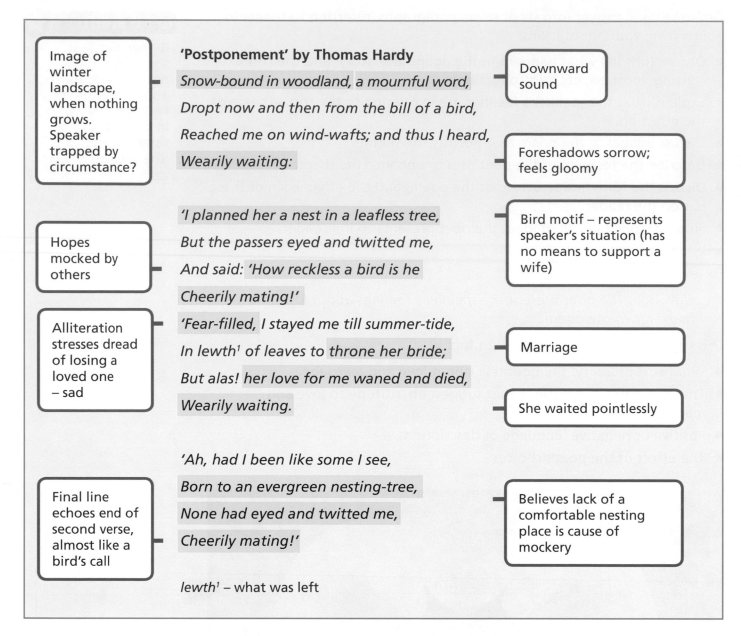

Techniques: Regular rhythm, **refrain** and full rhyme emphasise the speaker's feelings of certainty about his circumstances.

Form: a **lyric poem**.

Story: The speaker is trapped in a wood at winter and waits for help to come. He hears a bird singing and imagines his own situation is like the bird's.

Overall picture:

- The speaker's situation is represented by the bird **motif** (an idea repeated throughout the poem).
- The speaker has no financial means to keep a wife. Born into a low social class, as represented by the bare tree.

The task refers to the love and marriage theme – here, love died because the loved one would wait no longer for the speaker's situation to improve.

The effect is to create a shift between feelings of jaunty hope (for love) and despair (at the reality of the situation).

EXAM FOCUS

Read this extract from a successful analysis of the poem. The annotations show some of the points that would earn it marks.

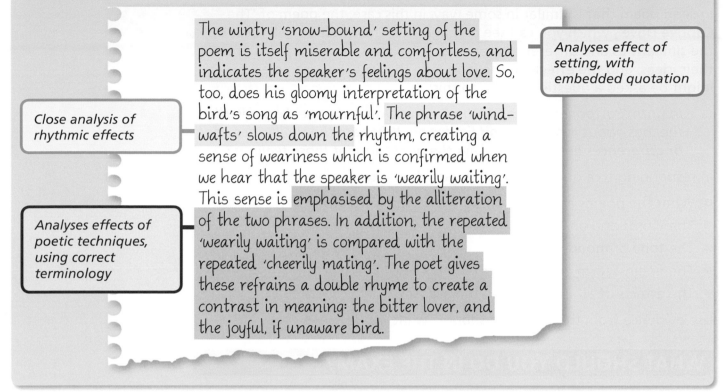

Close analysis of rhythmic effects

Analyses effects of poetic techniques, using correct terminology

The wintry 'snow-bound' setting of the poem is itself miserable and comfortless, and indicates the speaker's feelings about love. So, too, does his gloomy interpretation of the bird's song as 'mournful'. The phrase 'wind-wafts' slows down the rhythm, creating a sense of weariness which is confirmed when we hear that the speaker is 'wearily waiting'. This sense is emphasised by the alliteration of the two phrases. In addition, the repeated 'wearily waiting' is compared with the repeated 'cheerily mating'. The poet gives these refrains a double rhyme to create a contrast in meaning: the bitter lover, and the joyful, if unaware bird.

Analyses effect of setting, with embedded quotation

Reread the poem above, then answer these questions:

❶ Explain how Hardy refers to the importance of money in marriage in this poem.

❷ Comment on how effective you find Hardy's use of the narrative voice in this poem.

APPLYING YOUR SKILLS

❸ Write a second paragraph to follow on from the one in the Exam Focus. Comment on how Hardy presents the speaker's feelings of regret and disappointment in the poem.

Remember:

- Focus on word choices and their effects.
- Notice the effects of rhythm on mood.

COMPARING UNSEEN POEMS

You will be asked to compare the first poem you analysed with another unseen poem that is similar in some way, in this case, the poem of 'The Captive Dove', which you can see on page 129. The question will focus on the similarities and differences between the poems, how the poets present their ideas, and the effects of the language they use. For example, you might be asked a question similar to this:

> In both 'Postponement' and 'The Captive Dove', the speakers describe feelings about loneliness and limitation. What are the similarities and/ or differences between the ways the poets present those feelings?

In responding to a question like this, you should compare:

- What the poems are about and the key ideas presented
- The words and images
- The **tone** or **mood**
- The poems' form and structure
- The effects of all the above on the reader

Use evidence from the poems to support what you say.

WHAT SHOULD YOU DO IN THE EXAM?

- First, underline the key words in the question.
- Read the second poem through once, without making notes but with the focus of the task in the back of your mind.
- Read it again, making notes, annotations and highlights around it, focusing on the similarities and differences between the two poems.
- Write your response.

COMPARING THE POEMS

The main similarity is that both poems express the speaker's feelings of loneliness and despair through description of a bird. They project human feelings onto the bird.

The main differences are:

- **First poem:** Tells a story of overhearing a bird speaking about his disappointed nest-building – his attempts to enter married life with no money to keep his wife. Poet makes more use of poetic techniques – varied rhythm, the rhyming **refrain**, and alliteration.
- **Second poem:** Poet imagines the dove having human feelings (e.g. despair) and interprets its cooing as a 'joyless moan', but does not make it speak. The poet uses fewer techniques, but creates a more believable picture of the bird.

'The Captive Dove' by Anne Brontë

Poor restless dove, I pity thee;
And when I hear thy plaintive moan,
I mourn for thy captivity,
And in thy woes forget mine own.

To see thee stand prepared to fly,
And flap those useless wings of thine,
And gaze into the distant sky,
Would melt a harder heart than mine.

In vain – in vain! Thou canst not rise:
Thy prison roof confines thee there;
Its slender wires delude thine eyes,
And quench thy longings with despair.

Oh, thou wert made to wander free
In sunny mead and shady grove,
And, far beyond the rolling sea,
In distant climes, at will to rove!

Yet, hadst thou but one gentle mate
Thy little drooping heart to cheer,
And share with thee thy captive state,
Thou couldst be happy even there.

Yes, even there, if, listening by,
One faithful dear companion stood,
While gazing on her full bright eye,
Thou mightst forget thy native wood.

But thou, poor solitary dove,
Must make, unheard, thy joyless moan;
The heart, that Nature formed to love,
Must pine, neglected, and alone.

Annotations (left side):

- Shows sympathy; linked by **alliteration** to 'moan'; like 'mournful' in Hardy
- **Onomatopoeia** in 'flap'; compare with Hardy's 'wind-wafts'
- Repetition emphasises lack of hope; compare with 'Wearily waiting' in Hardy
- Again gives dove human feelings
- Personifies Nature

Annotations (right side):

- Subjectively interprets the dove's cooing as a 'moan'
- Speaker reveals own standpoint: sympathy helps her forget own unhappiness
- **Emotive language**, giving dove human feelings – like Hardy's bird
- Pictures happiness dove ought to have – like Hardy's final stanza
- Romantic view of possible happiness – like Hardy's 'throne her bride'

'Story': Speaker observes a dove in a cage and sympathises with its captivity and its lack of a mate.

Speaker's point of view: Deeply sympathetic, possibly identifying with the bird.

Form: Stanzas of regular iambic quadrameter, rhymed ABAB.

Structure: The poet pities the dove's attempts to fly, reflects on the freedom it ought to have, comments that it could still be happy if only it had a mate, and finally says that it is doomed to remain alone and unhappy.

EXAM FOCUS

Read this beginning to a successful response to the question. Some of its qualities have been highlighted:

> Both poems focus on a bird to explore feelings of loneliness and limitation. However, in Hardy there is a stronger sense of narrative, with a gloomy winter creating an appropriate mood, and the poet making the bird speak in very human terms, with the 'leafless tree' symbolising lack of money. In Brontë the bird seems more real, as with the realistic verb 'flap', but it is still given human feelings such as 'despair'.

Comparative link word introduces evaluative comparison

Analysis with correct term

Strong statement on key similarity

Evaluative comparison with evidence, qualified ('but ...')

APPLYING YOUR SKILLS

❶ Use the annotated notes and guidance to write a further paragraph building on the response in the Exam Focus. Remember to compare the styles of the two poems and their effects.

Remember:

- Compare the styles of the two poems.
- Compare the effects of the two poems.

PROGRESS CHECK FOR CHAPTER 11

GOOD PROGRESS

I can:

- Explain the methods poets use and understand the context of the poem ☐
- Comment on an 'unseen' poem, clearly referring to a range of techniques ☐
- Explain the similarities and differences between two poems ☐

EXCELLENT PROGRESS

I can:

- Analyse the methods poets use and the context of the poem. ☐
- Interpret an 'unseen' poem, selecting apt and precise evidence and referring to a wide range of techniques ☐
- Write a convincing and analytical comparison of two poems. ☐

CHAPTER 12: GCSE English Literature practice papers

PAPER 1, SECTION A: EXTRACT QUESTIONS ON SHAKESPEARE

In this chapter, locate the literature texts you are studying and answer the questions. Refer to the first page of the relevant chapter to remind yourself of the AOs assessed and the time allowed.

MACBETH

> Read *Macbeth* Act 3 Scene 4, from 'Avaunt! and quit my sight!' to 'I am a man again. Pray you, sit still', then answer the question that follows.

At this point in the play Macbeth and his wife are holding a banquet. Macbeth is speaking to the ghost of Banquo.

Starting with this section, explore how Shakespeare presents Macbeth's strengths and weaknesses.

Write about:

- How Shakespeare presents Macbeth in this speech
- How Shakespeare presents Macbeth in the play as a whole

ROMEO AND JULIET

> Read *Romeo and Juliet* Act 4 Scene 3, from 'Alack, alack, is it not like ...' to the end of the scene, and then answer the question that follows.

At this point in the play Juliet is alone in the Capulet vault.

Starting with this section, explore how Shakespeare engages our sympathies with Juliet.

Write about:

- How Shakespeare presents Juliet in this speech
- How Shakespeare presents Juliet in the play as a whole

THE TEMPEST

> Read *The Tempest* Act 1 Scene 2, from Prospero's words 'Thou most lying slave ...' to 'Who hadst deserved more than a prison', and then answer the question that follows.

At this point in the play Prospero and Miranda are outside Caliban's cave. Prospero is addressing Caliban.

Starting with this conversation, explain how far you think Shakespeare presents Prospero as using his power for the good.

Write about:

- How Shakespeare presents Prospero at this point in the play
- How Shakespeare presents Prospero in the play as a whole

PAPER 1, SECTION A: EXTRACT QUESTIONS ON SHAKESPEARE

THE MERCHANT OF VENICE

> Read *The Merchant of Venice* Act 3 Scene 1, from Salarino's words 'Why, I am sure, if he forfeit ...' to Shylock 'I will better the instruction', and then answer the question that follows.

At this point in the play Shylock is discussing his contract with Antonio.

Starting with this conversation, explore how Shakespeare presents the theme of revenge.

Write about:

- How Shakespeare presents the theme of revenge at this point in the play
- How Shakespeare presents the theme in the play as a whole

MUCH ADO ABOUT NOTHING

> Read *Much Ado About Nothing* Act 1 Scene 1, from Beatrice's words 'I wonder that you will still be talking' to 'You always end with a jade's trick: I know you of old', and then answer the question that follows.

At this point in the play Beatrice and Benedick have just met up again after some time.

Starting with this conversation, explain how far you think Shakespeare presents Beatrice and Benedick as suitable marriage partners for each other.

Write about:

- How Shakespeare presents the two characters at this point in the play
- How Shakespeare presents them in the play as a whole

JULIUS CAESAR

> Read *Julius Caesar* Act 1 Scene 2, from Cassius's words 'Why, man, he doth bestride ...' to 'But it was famed with more than with one man?', and then answer the question that follows.

At this point in the play Cassius is speaking to Brutus against Caesar's growing power.

Starting with this speech, explore how Shakespeare presents the theme of fate and free will.

Write about:

- How Shakespeare presents the them of fate in this conversation
- How Shakespeare presents the theme in the play as a whole

PAPER 1, SECTION B: EXTRACT QUESTIONS ON THE NINETEENTH-CENTURY NOVEL

ROBERT LOUIS STEVENSON: *THE STRANGE CASE OF DR JEKYLL AND MR HYDE*

Read Chapter 3, from 'The large handsome face of Dr Jekyll ...' to the end of the paragraph beginning 'Well, but since we have touched upon this business ...', and then answer the question that follows.

In this extract, Mr Utterson has just raised the subject of Jekyll's will, and offered to help him.

Starting with this extract, how far does Stevenson encourage readers to sympathise with Dr Jekyll?

Write about:

● How Stevenson presents Dr Jekyll in this extract
● How far Stevenson presents Dr Jekyll as someone we might sympathise with in the novella as a whole

CHARLES DICKENS: *A CHRISTMAS CAROL*

Read Chapter 4, from 'Still the Ghost pointed downward ...' to the end of the chapter, and then answer the question that follows.

In this extract, Scrooge is with the Ghost of Christmas Yet To Come.

Starting with this extract, explore how Dickens presents the process of Scrooge's transformation as a character.

Write about:

● How Dickens presents Scrooge changing in this extract
● How Dickens presents Scrooge changing in the novella as a whole

CHARLES DICKENS: *GREAT EXPECTATIONS*

Read Chapter 54, from 'You have a returned Transport there,' to the end of the paragraph beginning 'It was but for an instant ...', and then answer the question that follows.

In this extract, Pip is in a rowing boat on the Thames, trying to get Magwitch on to a steamer.

Starting with this extract, explore how Dickens creates suspense and drama.

Write about:

● How Dickens creates suspense and drama in this extract
● How Dickens creates suspense and drama in the novel as a whole

PAPER 1, SECTION B: EXTRACT QUESTIONS ON THE NINETEENTH-CENTURY NOVEL

CHARLOTTE BRONTË: *JANE EYRE*

> Read Chapter 4, from 'Psalms are not interesting,' to the end of the paragraph beginning 'Deceit is, indeed, a sad fault in a child', and then answer the question that follows.

In this extract, Jane is being questioned by Mr Brocklehurst at Lowood School.

Starting with this extract, explore how Brontë presents the difficulties and challenges that Jane faces.

Write about:

- How Brontë presents Jane's difficulties in this extract
- How Brontë presents the difficulties and challenges that Jane faces in the novel as a whole

MARY SHELLEY: *FRANKENSTEIN*

> Read Chapter 15, from 'I continued to wind among the paths of the wood' to the end of the paragraph beginning 'This was then the reward of my benevolence!', and then answer the question that follows.

In this extract, the Creature is telling Victor Frankenstein about the life he has lived so far.

Starting with this extract, explore how far Shelley presents the Creature as a victim.

Write about:

- How Shelley presents the Creature as a victim in this extract
- How Shelley presents the Creature in the novel as a whole

JANE AUSTEN: *PRIDE AND PREJUDICE*

> Read Chapter 22, from 'Why should you be surprised, my dear Eliza?' to the end of the chapter, and then answer the question that follows.

In this extract, Charlotte Lucas has just told Elizabeth that she is engaged to Mr Collins.

Starting with this extract, explore how Austen presents attitudes towards love and marriage.

Write about:

- How Austen presents attitudes towards love and marriage in this extract
- How Austen presents attitudes towards love and marriage in the novel as a whole

PAPER 1, SECTION B: EXTRACT QUESTIONS ON THE NINETEENTH-CENTURY NOVEL

SIR ARTHUR CONAN DOYLE: *THE SIGN OF THE FOUR*

Read from the start of Chapter 4 ('We followed the Indian down ...') to 'This is Mr Sherlock Holmes, and this is Dr Watson', and then answer the question that follows.

Starting with this extract, explore how Conan Doyle presents Thaddeus Sholto as an unusual and exotic character:

Write about:

- How Conan Doyle presents Thaddeus Sholto in this extract
- How Conan Doyle presents Thaddeus Sholto in the novel as a whole

PAPER 2, SECTION A: MODERN PROSE AND DRAMA

J. B. PRIESTLEY: *AN INSPECTOR CALLS*

What is the role of the Inspector in *An Inspector Calls*?

Write about:

- How the Inspector behaves towards the other characters
- How Priestley presents the Inspector by the ways he writes

WILLY RUSSELL: *BLOOD BROTHERS*

How and why does Russell contrast the lives and characters of Mickey and Edward?

Write about:

- How Russell presents Mickey and Edward
- What ideas Russell explores by comparing these characters

ALAN BENNETT: *THE HISTORY BOYS*

How does Bennett use the characters Hector and Irwin to explore ideas about education?

Write about:

- How Bennett presents the characters of Hector and Irwin
- How Bennett uses Hector and Irwin to explore ideas about education

PAPER 2, SECTION A: MODERN PROSE AND DRAMA

DENNIS KELLY: *DNA*

How does Kelly explore the theme of bullying?

Write about:

- How Kelly presents characters who are bullied, or who bully others
- How Kelly uses these characters to explore ideas about bullying

SIMON STEPHENS: *THE CURIOUS INCIDENT OF THE DOG IN THE NIGHT-TIME*

How does Stephens present the ways Christopher relates to other people?

Write about:

- How Christopher relates to other people
- How Stephens presents Christopher's relationships

SHELAGH DELANEY: *A TASTE OF HONEY*

How does Delaney explore the theme of love and marriage?

Write about:

- Attitudes towards love and marriage in the play
- How Delaney presents love and marriage by the way she writes

WILLIAM GOLDING: *LORD OF THE FLIES*

Compare the leadership styles of Ralph and Jack.

Write about:

- How Golding presents the characters of Ralph and Jack
- How Golding explores ideas about leadership in the way he writes about Ralph and Jack

AQA ANTHOLOGY: *TELLING TALES*

How do writers present relationships between adults and children in 'Odour of Chrysanthemums' and one other story from the collection?

Write about:

- Some of the ideas about adult–child relationships presented in the stories
- How the writers present these ideas by the way they write

PAPER 2, SECTION A: MODERN PROSE AND DRAMA

GEORGE ORWELL: *ANIMAL FARM*

How does Orwell use characters to explore ideas about the abuse of power?

Write about:

- How some characters abuse power
- How Orwell presents the abuse of power by the way he writes

KAZUO ISHIGURO: *NEVER LET ME GO*

How does Ishiguro present attitudes towards duty and obedience?

Write about:

- How Ishiguro uses different characters to present ideas about duty and obedience
- How Ishiguro presents these ideas by the ways he writes

MEERA SYAL: *ANITA AND ME*

How does Syal present the ways in which Meena changes during the course of the novel?

Write about:

- How Syal presents Meena's development as a character
- How Meena's development is influenced by other characters, and by events

STEPHEN KELMAN: *PIGEON ENGLISH*

How does Kelman present ideas about immigration and culture?

Write about:

- What we learn about how Harrison's adapts to life in London
- How Kelman presents Harrison's experience of immigration by the ways he writes

PAPER 2, SECTION B: COMPARING ANTHOLOGY POEMS

Compare how poets present relationships between children and their parents in 'Mother Any Distance' and one other poem from the 'Love and relationships' cluster.

Or

Compare how poets present ideas about conflict in 'Bayonet Charge' and one other poem from the 'Power and conflict' cluster.

PAPER 2, SECTION C: UNSEEN POETRY

Answer **both** questions in this section.

> **'It Rains'**
>
> It rains, and nothing stirs within the fence
> Anywhere through the orchard's untrodden, dense
> Forest of parsley. The great diamonds
> Of rain on the grassblades there is none to break,
> Or the fallen petals further down to shake.
>
> And I am nearly as happy as possible
> To search the wilderness in vain though well,
> To think of two walking, kissing there,
> Drenched, yet forgetting the kisses of the rain:
>
> Sad, too, to think that never, never again,
> Unless alone, so happy shall I walk
> In the rain. When I turn away, on its fine stalk
> Twilight has fined to naught, the parsley flower
> Figures, suspended still and ghostly white,
> The past hovering as it revisits the light.
>
> Edward Thomas

❶ In 'It Rains', how does the poet use the weather and the setting to express the speaker's feelings?

'The Voice'

Woman much missed, how you call to me, call to me,
Saying that now you are not as you were
When you had changed from the one who was all to me,
But as at first, when our day was fair.

Can it be you that I hear? Let me view you, then,
Standing as when I drew near to the town
Where you would wait for me: yes, as I knew you then,
Even to the original air-blue gown!

Or is it only the breeze, in its listlessness
Travelling across the wet mead to me here,
You being ever dissolved to wan wistlessness,
Heard no more again far or near?

Thus I; faltering forward,
Leaves around me falling,
Wind oozing thin through the thorn from norward,
And the woman calling.

Thomas Hardy

❷   In both 'It Rains' and 'The Voice' the poets describe their feelings
about a past relationship. What are the similarities and differences
between the ways the poets present these feelings.

CHAPTER 1

GRAMMATICAL TERMS [p. 6]

1 *We were all sitting on the harbour wall, watching the boats sail by, when suddenly a cry went up. 'Man overboard!', someone called. There was a terrific crack and I saw a huge wooden mast fall from a yacht. It crashed into the sea near where a man in a yellow lifejacket was floundering around. I called out in disbelief, 'That's my dad!'*

2

Nouns		Pronouns	Verbs		Adjectives
common	proper		auxiliary	main	
hat	London	I	have	see	big
book	Saturday	who	will	book	**happy**
table	Italy	**his**	**may**	**go**	**responsible**
actor	April	**himself**		**make**	**tall**
		you		**run**	
		me			

Adverbs	Determiners	Prepositions	Conjunctions	
			coordinating	subordinating
quickly	the	of	or	because
together	**his**	to	**and**	**while**
sharply	**my/your**	on	**but**	**although**
soon	**a/an**	in		**if**

3 For example: 'university teacher', 'cream tea'.

4 ***Uncle Ray's rabbit in the hutch*** *is snoring.*

The small boy *was* ***a lost and bewildered newcomer***.

5 *She's annoyed* ***because of the holiday cancellation***. (adverbial – shows the relationship between 'annoyed' and 'cancellation').

It seems the robin ***on the windowsill*** *visits daily.* (adjectival – shows the relationship between the robin and the windowsill).

SENTENCE CONSTRUCTION AND CLAUSES [p. 8]

1 Simple sentence; minor sentence; compound sentence

2 'because they need money'; 'in order to cultivate the coca plant'; 'While tribespeople use rainforest resources'

3 Examples:

Jake always ate well ***because*** *he was a great chef,* ***who*** *cooked at home.*

Although *Sian had a strong voice, she didn't practise enough* ***because*** *she had too much to do.*

Having *finished work, Kai,* ***who*** *loved sky-diving, had training* ***and*** *practised his skills.*

SENTENCE TYPES AND TENSES [p. 10]

1 Suggested starters: 'The geese are …'; 'The book of rules is …'; 'Kate or Jack is …'; 'Either of the acrobats is …'; 'Neither of the clowns are …'

2 *A series of hits was performed by the rapper.*

Her intentions were declared. ('by her' not needed.)

The result was anticipated by Danny and Marlon.

3 *I* ***was*** *the first to get home on Wednesday, so I* ***made*** *myself a cup of cappuccino with our new coffee maker. It* ***does*** *you good to relax sometimes. It* ***wasn't*** *for long though, because five minutes later there* ***was*** *a loud banging on the door. When I* ***opened*** *it I* ***saw*** *my little brother* ***standing*** *there, sinking under the weight of his schoolbag, with tears streaming down his face.*

PUNCTUATION [p. 12]

1 Answers will vary.

2 *Mr Bennet told his family that about a month ago he received a letter and answered it about a fortnight later, since he thought it was a matter of some delicacy that needed early attention. It was from his cousin, Mr Collins, who, when Mr Bennet was dead, could turn the whole family out of the house as soon as he pleased.*

PARAGRAPH ORGANISATION [p. 15]

1 *Exceptionally heavy rain …* (as given)

In addition, rail and property …

Finally, heavy rain is expected …

SPELLING [p. 16]

1 Corrected spellings: 'heroes', 'countries', 'valleys', 'libraries', 'roofs', 'dreadful', 'irrigation', 'advantageous'.

Exceptions: 'motifs'.

Literary terms: 'parodies', 'motifs', 'ironies', 'paradoxes', 'ambiguities'.

2 Answers will vary.

3 Corrected spellings: 'losing', 'pieces', 'fibrous', 'tied', 'knot', 'seen', 'until', 'break', 'threw', 'higher'.

homophones spelled incorrectly: 'tied', 'knot', 'seen', 'break', 'threw', 'higher'.

Homophones spelled correctly: 'time', 'two', 'not', 'to', 'one', 'missed'.

CHAPTER 2

FINDING EXPLICIT INFORMATION [p. 20]

1 It is a hot afternoon. There are two small girls, a small boy, their aunt and a man they do not know in the carriage. The children and their aunt talk to each other and the children ask lots of questions.

2 The 'next stop' is at Templecombe, but there is no mention of the children and aunt getting off.

3 The child does not want to move to the window. They pass fields of sheep and cattle. The aunt attempts to answer the child's question. The bachelor is beginning to scowl.

FINDING IMPLICIT INFORMATION [p. 22]

1 The girl may be bored and want to distract the aunt. The girl is determined. The girl likes the poem but not enough to learn it all.

2 The bachelor sees the likelihood of the girl continuing in terms of a 'bet', a 'wager'. This suggests that he is familiar with betting, and that he has the time, money and inclination to make bets like this himself.

3 The children do not want to hear the aunt's story. The aunt does not want to irritate the bachelor further by telling the story. The aunt is a poor storyteller. The bachelor listens to the story and is critical of it.

QUOTING OR PARAPHRASING EFFECTIVELY [p. 24]

1 Strong, decisive character: 'imperious mien', 'definite black eyebrows', 'parted exactly', 'calm and set'.

Reason to be unhappy: 'disillusionment'.

2 For example: *The fact that the mother speaks 'distinctly' shows that she knows her son can hear her and expects him to answer her; Her looking 'piercingly' suggests that she is a strict and vigilant mother whose children cannot easily get away with misbehaviour.*

3 For example: *The boy is five years old, small but well built. He likes playing by the brook and is 'defiantly' reluctant to come home, even to please his mother.*

ANALYSING LANGUAGE FEATURES AND EFFECTS [p. 26]

1 'bounding', 'running', 'great roar', 'vast deafening snarl'.

2 'Bounding' and 'running' suggest urgency; 'great roar' and 'vast deafening snarl' suggest a noise like a savage, dangerous animal.

3 The repetition of 'too lazy' emphasises Yvette's idleness, almost as if she cannot be bothered to think of another phrase. 'Strayed' and 'dreamy' suggest purposeless wandering.

4 Simile ('like a wet, shuddering cat'); personification ('the water raved').

5 The simile makes her sound like an animal, as if she is reduced to the level of animal survival, while 'shuddering' emphasises her physical response to fear and trauma. The personification presents the water as a 'raving' mad person, who cannot be reasoned with.

6 For example: *The simple verb 'gone' suggests the shock of finding the bridge simply swept away. The simile personifying the house as leaning as if making a bow makes it sound like a person acknowledging the power of the water. The nouns 'wreckage' and 'debris' suggest the high level of destruction, while the personification of 'gaping mouths' for the now empty rooms suggests mouths gaping in horror, or even death.*

ANALYSING THE EFFECTS OF DIFFERENT TYPES OF SENTENCES [p. 30]

1 Compound ('The pack ice seemed to have closed and the ship ...'); minor ('Nothing for it').

2 The compound sentence links the fact and its consequence as if they are inseparable. The minor sentence expresses the Captain's grim resignation to the loss.

3 A simple sentence makes a dramatic opening. Grammatical inversion (instead of saying, 'It happened just before nightfall') delays the event, creating drama. The complex sentences 'Although ...' and 'Grabbing ...' also delay the information, building suspense by suggesting danger first. Two short simple sentences create a sense of urgency. A longer one suggests the size of the bear. Finally, a dramatic simple sentence reveals the nature of the danger.

ANALYSING THE STRUCTURE OF A TEXT [p. 32]

1 A The men are fixated on the fast-moving, rough sea, probably because they are worried about their situation. The grey sea, reflecting the sky, suggests bad weather.

B It is winter and the weather is bad. The narrator and others are 'wandering', suggesting purposeless exercise on a cold wintry day.

C Suggests that marriage and money will be key themes. The statement could be ironic, as not all unmarried and wealthy men are looking for a wife.

2 A How did the men get into this situation? Will they survive?

B Why are the children wandering about in the cold? Who is Mrs Reed? What will the narrator and the other wanderers do now?

C Does the author really believe that this is a 'universal truth'. Is she about to introduce a wealthy male character and some possible wives?

3 For example: *This reveals more of the narrator's character: she is a child, is not an 'outdoor type', and feels physically weak. She seems unhappy – told off by Bessie, and excluded from the group of children. She refers to 'their mama', implying that Mrs Reed is mother to three children, but not the narrator – perhaps why she is excluded, which begins to win our sympathy. The mother seems content, pampered and perhaps lazy.*

4 For example: *The waggoner leaves; What is on the wagon; What the girl does.*

5 For example: *Hardy creates atmosphere with the 'stillness' – apart from the canary. He makes the package seem significant by describing it without* saying what it is. He implies that the girl is tempted to do something that she does not want the waggoner to see. Her smiling at herself implies that she is secretly vain.

6 For example: *Brontë uses parallel sentences to emphasise the contrast between the pair: 'He wanted all to ... I wanted all to ...'; 'I said his ... He said mine ...'. The sentences become shorter, indicating a rise in tension as Cathy and Linton come close to falling out.*

FORMING AN INTERPRETATION: EVALUATING A TEXT [p. 36]

1 For example: *The writer also reveals that the narrator is contradictory in another way: he dislikes work but appreciates that it is character-building.*

2 See Exam Focus, page 39.

3 What characters do: Errol looks at his watch and drums his fingers (shows his anxiety).

Descriptive language: 'haunted face creasing' (shows anxiety, strain).

Detail: 'stuffed owl' is unsettling.

Ideas: Errol's sense of being 'trapped' makes the reader wonder who or what is trapping him.

4 Errol's repeated glances at his watch and his drumming on the table [Evidence] are effective ways to show that he is tensely waiting for something, [Analysis and evaluation] revealing his anxious nature. [Point]

5 For example: *A persuasive sense of menace is created by the adjectives 'trapped, vulnerable', and the strong verb 'glaring', which all imply threat, showing that the character feels in danger.*

6 For example: *The author makes us imagine the narrator's experience in several ways. He uses repetition of 'trees' and a list of adjectives to convey the overpowering nature of the forest. The description of the steamboat 'hugging the bank', makes it, and the man, sound insecure, as if threatened, and 'little begrimed' emphasises how small human beings are compared with this environment. The simile of the boat being like a 'small ... grimy beetle' in a big hallway adds to this sense of overwhelming size. At the same time, the boat 'crawled on', so we see the man is not completely overwhelmed.*

7 For example: *The mood of the extract is one of combined horror and mystery. The narrator is 'chilled and horrified' but can only strain 'to listen through the mist'. The mist creates a sense of mystery and prevents him from seeing what is happening, and so he relies on the frightening evidence of sounds, which are vividly described: 'draining, sucking, churning'. In a way, the effect is intensified by it being*

reduced to one sense. The author creates a strong sense of the narrator feeling 'absolutely helpless' and feeling intense 'frustration'. The fact that a child seems to be dying makes the experience traumatic.

CHAPTER 3

EFFECTIVE DESCRIPTIVE WRITING [p. 42]

1 Rain trickling from caps and hoods; streets and boulevards; umbrellas; cars.

2 Rain 'assaulted meagre streets'; umbrellas 'collapsed from exhaustion'.

3 Powerful verbs – 'drenched', 'streamed', 'squelched'; vivid adjectives – 'waterlogged', 'miserable'; repetition – 'water streamed ... Water ran ... waterlogged'; other vocabulary choices – 'Rivulets'.

4 Answers will vary.

5 Answers will vary.

CREATING ATMOSPHERE AND MOOD [p. 44]

1 Alarm, horror, fear.

2 Questions: *'And this Thing I saw? How can I describe it?'*; semicolon, commas: 'career; a walking engine' and several commas; short sentences followed by a long one: opening two short sentences followed by a long one.

3 Rhetorical questions: viewpoint; contemplate the unanswerable; emphasis.

4 Exclamation mark and full stops after minor sentences.

5 Answers will vary.

GENERATING IDEAS AND STRUCTURING A DESCRIPTION [p. 46]

1 Answers will vary.

2 For example: *The speeding express train was crammed full of tired commuters when it happened.*

3 For example:
- *The <u>glowing</u> fairground lights, which <u>drew her like a moth</u>, twinkled <u>and dazzled</u> in the dark.*
- *They walked <u>in mournful silence</u> along the <u>windswept</u> beach for the last time.*
- *The <u>brand new</u> laptop, <u>with which he had been so delighted</u>, had been completely dismantled.*

4 Answers will vary.

CREATING CONVINCING CHARACTERS AND VOICES [p. 48]

1 For example: *She seems a strong, possibly stubborn character, resistant to persuasion.*

2 For example: *She seems to be very sure of herself, and determined to resist the new road. She regards the officer as a minor difficulty. She seems blunt – taking him literally and simply refusing to move.*

3 For example: *She stood in the kitchen, dark eyes glaring at her father, arms tightly folded, bright red nails digging into her upper arm.*

'I don't see why you need to know where I'm going. I don't even know myself. I'm meeting Kylie – that's all. Anyway, why do you care all of a sudden?'

4 Joe seems heroic in the third-person version, but rather vain in the first-person.

5 Answers will vary.

GENERATING IDEAS AND STRUCTURING A NARRATIVE [p. 50]

1–3 Answers will vary.

4 For example: *David hauled the faded, velvet armchair through the rickety gate and swung the gate shut with his right boot. It shuddered on its hinges. He grinned. That stain on the armrest was where Cherry had spilt her coffee the evening he'd proposed to her. She'd been shocked into silence for ten seconds, then flung herself at him. They'd been married in spring, in the church on the edge of the moors. She'd looked as pretty as the crocuses that lined the path. How quickly things had changed ... His reverie was interrupted by a creak on the stairs behind him. He turned – to face a man in a balaclava. He held a gun.*

CHAPTER 4

IDENTIFYING CORRECT INFORMATION [p. 56]

1 No. She read 'all the names you'd expect to see on the list' – well-known authors.

2 B, C, E, G

3 B, C, F, H

SUMMARISING AND SYNTHESISING FROM TWO TEXTS [p. 58]

1 Evidence for attitudes in Source A:
- *Abandonment. Helplessness. Pain, loss and grief. These are the big things that frighten us ... These are the new sabre-tooth tigers.*
- *a spear is going to make you feel a lot better about your odds of survival*
- *Horror stories reflect their times.*

2 Examples of attitudes in Source B:
- *Children cannot cope with frightening stories: these stories create unmanageable fears.*
- *All children are as frightened by frightening*

stories as each other, and get ill because of them.

- *The experience of nature helps children to overcome fears.*
- *Children's books should not copy adult novels.*
- *Children are made for joy and laughter, not fears or threats.*

3 For example:

In Morgan's opinion, in the past fear has played an important part in human survival. However, she says that people's fears now tend to be more abstract, such as fear of abandonment. She feels that horror fiction and other fiction focusing on fear and danger can help us cope with our fears by presenting them in a manageable way. In addition, these stories reflect the fears of the time in which they are written.

Osborne, on the other hand, writing about children's reading, considers that children's stories should not attempt to copy adult fiction. Nor should they set out to frighten children into moral behaviour. Moreover, books that do this are likely to make children anxious, sleepless and even ill. He thinks that children's books should promote joy and laughter rather than fear and sadness.

UNDERSTANDING PERSUASIVE LANGUAGE [p. 60]

1 'dreams and screams': rhyming is apt in a text about children, but also emphasises how wrong it is to scare them, because 'dreams' should be innocent and positive; 'all kinds of intestinal torture': alliteration adds impact, helping to create grimly humorous exaggeration, as if doctors are torturing children in various ways; 'intoxicating literature': compares stories with alcohol, even poison.

2 Possible points: Opens with rhetorical question effectively comparing 'food' for body and brain, suggesting that we should see them in the same way. Use of 'we' draws in the reader. Uses metaphor effectively in 'rubbing off the natural angles' and 'wrapping up'. 'Dumb animals and their young' sums up his view of what appeals to children in a way that will faintly amuse adult readers. 'I never fear ...' makes a point that is persuasive because it makes obvious sense. The final sentence uses a semicolon to make two linked, balanced points. The second appeals to adults because they will identify with the idea that in adulthood we have to accept 'sorrow'.

COMPARING WRITERS' VIEWPOINTS AND TECHNIQUES [p. 62]

1 Source A techniques and effects:

- Light-hearted phrase 'my corner of Twitter' (Twitter is not a place) flags up the 'unscientific' nature of the 'survey'. Listing modern fears (e.g. 'Pain, loss and grief') emphasises their extent. Repetition of 'These' in two sentences is powerful, as is turning 'sabre-tooth tigers' into a metaphor.
- Makes readers picture themselves 'faced with a sabre-tooth tiger'.
- Asks two questions about coping with fear, and then answers 'Simple' (effective minor sentence).
- Onomatopoeia and metaphor to describe fear in 'so much of it sloshing around in our heads that we drown in it'.
- Metaphor of 'pocket' or 'box' in a story that we can fill with our fears.
- Lists modern sources of anxiety: 'technology, zombies, dystopia and psychological terrors'.
- Effective return to personal anecdote in final paragraph, with 'fear of not being able to trust your own mind' earning our respect.

Comparison:

- Both use personal anecdote (Morgan's teenage book-buying; Osborne's picking up a children's book). Morgan more humorous ('sabre-tooth tigers', etc.).
- Both use lists: Morgan lists horror authors and modern fears; Osborne lists frightening features illustrated in the children's book.
- Morgan asks questions, then answers them herself; Osborne uses a rhetorical question in the final paragraph to emphasise that it is time we took more care with children's literature.
- Morgan uses colloquial but effective metaphor ('sloshing around ...'); Osborne uses metaphor less obviously ('rubbing off ... wrapping up').
- Morgan uses the deliberately clichéd image of the 'sabre-tooth tiger' to sum up primitive dangers and fears; Osborne is more visual and original in listing frightening features of the children's book: 'awful owls with eyes of fire'.

2 Headings might be: 'The terrifying children's book'; 'How frightening books make children ill and nature cures them'; 'Children's book should be joyful, not frightening'.

3 A high-level response should be in fluent prose, using connectives where appropriate and should combine:

- Comparison of attitudes
- Comparison of style and techniques (see answer to Question 1 above)
- Comparison of structure (see Question 2 above)

CHAPTER 5

WHAT IS WRITING TO EXPRESS A VIEWPOINT? [p. 66]

1 Zoos: purpose = explain views; audience = educated readers interested in topical issues; form = weekend magazine article (audience will have leisure to read it in detail, but may want to be entertained as well as informed).

Television: purpose = influence, persuade; audience = informed media professionals; form = speech (so might make more use of rhetoric than an article).

2 The second is more formal. Vocabulary: 'colleagues', 'appreciate', 'provide ... adequate facilities', 'maximise our efficiency', etc.

The second is more persuasive, despite being too formal. For example, it could say 'have to come out on strike'.

3 Purpose = explain views, persuade; audience = internet users interested in social media; form = blog.

Example sentences: *Endangered elephants, dolphins, the blue whale – you name it, I've done my bit to save it. Am I a dedicated environmental activist, prepared to put in time and effort to protect the planet and my fellow creatures? Er ... sort of – that is, I will happily fill in the first letter of my email address so that the rest pops up for me to sign an online petition.*

KEY FEATURES OF NON-FICTION TEXTS EXPRESSING A VIEWPOINT [p. 68]

1 For example: *Who wants to look like someone washed up on the shores of an island called 'Out of Touch'? Not me. I've got the right trainers, the right jeans, the right sweatshirt. You, of course, might say that I have the wrong views, the wrong priorities, the wrong attitude, but face it, you'd be in a miserable minority.*

2 For example: *I took my little sister Mandy to the park the other day. She was proudly wearing her new jeans. While there, we saw a teenage girl also wearing brand new jeans. The difference was that hers had slashes carefully cut into them. 'Look at her,' said Mandy. 'I bet she wishes she had nice jeans like mine.' And to me, five-year-old Mandy has the right idea.*

3 For example: *Hoodies, heels or horrendous haircuts: everyone seems to feel a need to make their personal style statement. But are they declaring their individuality or announcing their stupidity? A few stars, like Gaga or Rita Ora, may make a statement, but everyone else looks around like lost sheep for someone to follow, and then plays safe.*

USING LANGUAGE TO ARGUE OR PERSUADE [p. 70]

1 Figurative language techniques:

- Simile. Sounds as if the economy is not under control and cannot easily be brought under control, which could be disastrous.
- Simile. Makes it clear that such a law is useless because a chocolate teapot would melt.
- Metaphor. Implies that some effort is needed to succeed through education.
- Personification. Makes war sound merciless and destructive.

2 For example:

- *School pupils all in their identical uniforms, like <u>a shoal of sardines</u>.* (simile)
- *She took to the job as easily as a <u>duck to water</u>.* (simile)
- *The <u>window</u> of opportunity opened and I <u>climbed through it</u>.* (metaphor)
- *The steady <u>march</u> of progress has transformed this community.* (personification)

3 For example:

- *This senseless new road will desecrate a part of our rural heritage.*
- *Many talented but unqualified school-leavers find themselves the victims of unemployment.*

4 For example: *Introducing a tax on sugary foods: According to the nursery rhyme, 'Sugar and spice and all things nice' are what little girls are made of, but for both girls and boys in today's society sugar is no innocent matter. More and more young children are visiting dentists with rotting and painful teeth caused by this supposedly simple pleasure. Sugar has become the curse of the young – hidden in supposedly healthy juice drinks and even savoury items like ketchup. It's time to highlight the damage done by this silent stalker by making it more expensive!*

USING DIFFERENT TYPES OF SENTENCES [p. 72]

1 Main: 'Owain plays for England'; subordinate: 'although he lives in Wales'.

Main: 'They are completely bilingual'; subordinate: 'Having been brought up in the UK'

Main: 'Switzerland gave women the vote only in 1990'; subordinate: 'which is advanced in many ways'.

2 Main: *They can barely find time to speak to each other in person.*

Alternative order: *They can barely find time to speak to each other in person, despite being addicted to the current favourites of my own peer group – Facebook, Snapchat and Instagram.*

3 For example: *We used to be limited to face-to-face communication – before social media apps became the new social glue, enabling us to talk to each other* in so many ways. With Facebook – so easy to use that even my granddad uses it – we can invite all our friends to a party in seconds. Some people talk about the threat of social media, pointing to cyber-bullying and terrorism. But any form of communication can be used for good or bad. The internet is a way to join our intelligences, turning us into one huge interconnected human mind – which could be the way forward for humanity.

USING PUNCTUATION TO PERSUADE [p. 74]

1 Punctuation:

- *Although many apps are free, downloading them uses up your data.*
- *It is free, simple to use, and readily available, and, what's more, it works.*

2 Comma after 'However' avoids confusion. Round brackets show that the reference to Ozzie is an optional extra. The question mark indicates a question.

3 Answers will vary.

USING STRUCTURES CREATIVELY [p. 76]

1 For example: *We will all need to speak to people, in and out of work, for the rest of our lives, but relatively few people will need to do a lot of writing. Therefore schools should focus on verbal communication, not written. It is often said that writing is a mark of civilisation. However, being able to express yourself verbally is far more useful. Moreover, verbal skills fulfil emotional needs: few of us make real friends just by writing to them. In short, schools are currently preparing us for exams, but not for life.*

2 Example plan:

- *We live in a democracy, and we need to be informed to take part in it.*
- *Being politically aware involves knowing about history.*
- *We need history to avoid the mistakes of the past and to plan a better future.*
- *We also need history to give us a sense of context – where we come from.*
- *Conclusion: we need more history in school, not less.*

3 Example opening paragraph: *Dear Governors, I feel that the move towards phasing out history in school is potentially disastrous. We live in a democracy, and for it to work properly, without it being hijacked by wealthy elites, we need to understand the trends and mistakes of history. Dictators like Hitler thrive on ignorance, which is why we need to study history in school.*

Example conclusion: *We live in ever more complicated times, when political questions often*

seem to be beyond the reach of the ordinary person. But whether we are contemplating leaving the EU or abandoning nuclear missiles, we cannot avoid our personal responsibility. This is why we need history – to help us choose politicians and policies that will promote peace, wealth and justice.

CHAPTER 6

PAPER 1 SECTION A: READING [p. 80]

1

- He is not a scientist.
- He does not seem to be someone who lives a healthy outdoor physical life.
- He is interested in the cholera bacillus.
- He is impressed by the destructive power of the bacillus.

2

- Emphasis on his paleness, 'deep grey eyes' suggesting a 'deep' character – an intellectual type, not e.g. a sportsman.
- Adjectives 'haggard', 'nervous' and 'fitful' suggest a mentally unwell person, perhaps unbalanced or obsessive, working too hard.
- His 'gleam of satisfaction' when he thinks of destruction is menacing, and his 'morbid' interest implies an unhealthy interest in death.
- 'devouring' – strong verb implying unhealthy interest in the bacillus, as if he cannot get enough of it.

3

- At the beginning the writer focuses on the bacillus itself – looks unimpressive, yet has huge destructive potential. Writer introduces the two men – scientist and visitor. Scientist is helpful and knowledgeable; visitor is mysterious, but seems to have an unhealthy interest in disease and death.
- Focus gradually shifts to the scientist's perception of the visitor, who is so unlike the down-to-earth fellow scientists he is used to. Physical description of visitor (a little vampire-like!) makes reader suspect him.
- Scientist taking 'the most effective aspect' implies that he is going to respond somehow to the visitor being so 'impressionable'.
- Scientist then does respond, dramatising the lethal potential of the bacillus, personifying it as if it is a villain that can be instructed to destroy human life. He tells a story of this 'criminal' bacillus destroying thousands of lives.

4

- The writer describes the scientist holding the tube 'thoughtfully', suggesting detached scientific interest. The scientist describes bacillus impartially as 'minute particles of life', treating it as a fact of life rather than simply an evil.

- Writer dramatises bacillus through the words of the bacteriologist. Use of 'pestilence' creates strong negative impression, emphasised by alliteration in the 'p' sound of 'imprisoned'.
- Use of 'Imprisoned' also subtly introduces personification of bacillus as a criminal who may be set loose to destroy.
- Scientist contrasts tiny size of bacillus with awful effects.
- 'Go forth and multiply' is a biblical phrase, so this suggests someone – perhaps the scientist – playing God, ordering the bacillus to destroy.
- Writer, through the scientist, creates a highly imaginative account of what would happen if the bacillus was released. Several adjectives emphasise the awful and unavoidable death that would result: 'mysterious, untraceable death, death swift and terrible'.
- Writer personalises the effects in 'husband from the wife', etc.
- Repetition of 'He would' creates powerful and personified sense of possible destruction.
- 'decimated the metropolis': strong verb-noun combination on which to end.

PAPER 1 SECTION B: WRITING [p. 83]

5 Write a description suggested by the picture.

Extract from a mid-level response

All around the laboratory there are men and women in crisp white coats looking at test tubes. They hold them up to the light, heat them over Bunsen burners, or compare them in little racks. The morning light come in through the high windows, but these scientists seem unaware of that. Their investigations take up all their attention. Some are frowning, as if there is some mystery that they just cannot understand.

In the centre of the room is a huge bubbling vat with a guard rail all around it and gleaming silver pipes coming out and going off in all directions, like a motorway junction. The steam gives off a horrible smell, like old socks, but everyone here seems to have got used to it. One man with lank black hair stands next to a collection of dials and, now and again he writes down figures from the dials in small handwriting in a big book. He smiles faintly sometimes, with a look of someone who is determined to do an experiment and thinks it is beginning to go well.

But the most interesting thing in the laboratory is what hangs overhead – an enormous tank full of a liquid that ripples like a rainbow. It catches the light and seems to shine brilliantly. If you stand close, you can hear it humming, like bees.

Comment

An organised response, with competent use of sentence structures and punctuation. There is some evidence of thoughtful word choice ('crisp', 'gleaming') and some fairly effective figurative language (like a 'rainbow'). There is some appeal to the senses. Paragraphs are used appropriately for shifts in focus.

A 'good' level response needs:
- More interesting and effective word choices to replace phrases such as 'horrible smell'
- More development of focus (e.g. could have focused in more on the man with lank hair)
- More detail (e.g. the faces of the scientists looking at test tubes)

Extract from a high-level response

The eager young researchers in their starched white coats stand in a huddle, concentrating hard on what they see through the elongated lens of the high-powered microscope. Tiny filaments of pink and blood red swirl and separate. Could this be the beginnings of new life – or the end of all life as we know it?

Zooming out from the focused group reveals a strange scene – one that resembles a cross between a zoo and a Victorian carnival freak show. In the corner, a cage of headless chickens strut around as if having no head was as normal as pecking corn – though of course they cannot do that. Nearby, a grotesque monstrosity of a baboon jabbers to itself – literally, because its two heads seem to be in conversation. Its fur is long, and unnaturally silky, like human hair. In the centre of the room an oblong tank is filled with dogfish – but not the ordinary kind: these are the horrific product of more scientific meddling, mixing the genes of a goldfish and a Labrador. A bored technician drops in weighted sticks, and the dogfish swims to fetch them.

But pride of place in this freak show goes to the cage at the centre of the room, where the huge figure of a human-like creature paces up and down like a caged lion, grunting in a way that cannot be understood. The stitches around his scalp and wrists show where his white-coated creators have recently assembled his parts to make something like themselves.

Comment

A well-crafted description, moving in a structured way from the scientists to their creations, climaxing in the attempt to create a human being. Effective use of descriptive language, with varied sentence types, and figurative language (e.g. 'a cross between ...'), and the rhetorical question at the end of the first paragraph.

A 'very high' level response needs:

- More connection between the scientists in paragraph 1 and the rest of the description
- Slightly more originality (e.g. 'like a caged lion' is a cliché and is too obvious)
- Some more effective word choices (e.g. 'in a way that cannot be understood' could be replaced by 'incoherently')

Write a story about a scientific experiment that goes wrong.

Extract from a mid-level response

Professor Jones – Tracy to her friends – was excited. This could be the making of her career. A degree in biochemistry, higher qualifications specialising in skin nutrition, and a special study in human ageing. Now she was the world expert in research into anti-ageing. She looked at herself in the mirror of the ladies' toilet. She was a thirty-year-old woman, brown-eyed, pretty but with very strong eyebrows. 'Could this be the face behind world-famous cosmetics?' she asked herself.

For four long years she had led research funded by Laboratory Dernier into what they called the 'holy grail' of cosmetics – a skin cream that would halt the ageing process. But she was an ambitious woman, so that wasn't enough. She wanted to reverse back the ageing process.

At last the time had come to begin the trials. Four women had volunteered and were going to be paid a shedload of money. There was a bit of a risk involved after all. All were over 60, wrinkled and saggy, way past their prime. But all hoped to be transformed – and not just financially.

On day one the women applied 'Factor X', the top-secret new preparation. They did it for a week. After a week they all looked a lot younger – perhaps by about ten years. After another week of treatment, the results were astonishing.

'I've been given a new lease of life,' one woman said. 'My husband hardly recognises me!'

After a further week of treatment, the women had teenage skin – smooth and tight, but without any spots. But that's when things started to go horribly wrong ...

Comment

An engaging response that sets up an imaginative and effective scenario with narrative potential. The candidate uses details and descriptive language to establish a believable character. There is some variety of sentence structure, and competent use of paragraphs. The device of having the character see herself in the mirror and speak to herself is effective.

A 'good' level response needs:

- A consistent register and tone (e.g. 'shedload' and 'bit of a risk' are too informal)
- More interesting and effective descriptive language
- Avoidance of accidental repetition (e.g. 'for a week. After a week ...').

Extract from a high-level response

Damian Scrupleforth was a remarkable baby. Smiling amiably at the world within a few days, crawling in a matter of weeks, and speaking his first words, quite distinctly, at two months: 'More formula milk, please.'

The 'please' was the cause of particular delight, because Damian had been designed to be polite and considerate at all times. At the government Alpha Project playgroup, where he played intelligent and character-building games with his fellow toddlers, Damian was politely assertive: 'I think you'll find that I was already playing with those Lego bricks, Robert.' This was when he had reached the age of two.

By the time Damian entered the choppy waters of the teenage years, he was doing quadratic equations, contributing to New Scientist magazine, and, of course, helping the elderly across the road. His physique was strong, and his health as sound as a bell. This was no surprise. He was, after all, a product of the latest twenty-first-century genetic engineering.

The first signs of it began when Damian turned fifteen. There was a girl who lived near the government compound that he called 'home'. She was just a 'normal', but somehow whenever he glimpsed her his heart fluttered like a caged canary, and his mouth went dry. One day she smiled at him in passing – a smile like the sun emerging from the clouds, and a symphony of sensations seemed to go through him. ...

Comment

The response shows a varied and inventive use of structural devices, including withholding information (e.g. who is delighted at his politeness). Sentences are varied and effective (e.g. opening with a short simple sentence, followed by a long minor one). Language devices are used well (e.g. groups of three such as 'solving quadratic equations ... road').

A 'very high' level response needs:

- More consistently interesting and effective word choices (e.g. 'go through him' could be 'flood through him')
- More descriptive detail (e.g. what he looks like)
- Avoidance of accidental repetition (e.g. 'polite ... politely' – could use 'courteous')

PAPER 2 SECTION A: READING [p. 84]

1 A, D, E, G

2

- Writer A, Alice Fisher, regards fashion as entertaining, though sometimes silly; calls celebrity styles 'vivid and fun'. Enjoys individuality of fashionable display.
- Writer B, George Bernard Shaw, has no objection to fashion being regulated, as by Covent Garden Opera. He sees this regulation as functional, but thinks it should apply to women as well as men.
- Fisher compares catwalk fashion with celebrity styles, saying the latter has become more 'outrageous', which she seems to enjoy.
- Shaw objects to the vulgarity of showy female fashion, and especially to the distasteful fashion of having dead birds or parts of them on hats. Thinks the public should be protected from shocking or offensive fashion.

3

- Presents himself as a reasonable man who accepts Covent Garden's rules for male clothing. Lists arguments supporting them.
- Uses this to launch a criticism of female fashion, using popular expression that reinforces view of himself as reasonable and normal – 'sauce for the goose ...'
- Uses anecdote – the woman in front of him.
- Uses ironic humour – 'I wish she had come later ...'
- 'pitiable corpse' emphasises reality of what it is – a dead bird, not just an accessory.
- Uses rhetorical question, followed by humour in exaggerated description of how he might appear – 'dead snake round my neck', etc.

4

- Fisher regards fashion as fun and interesting, even if not of 'vast cultural significance'.
- Shaw sees no virtue in fashion, focusing on the offence it can cause.
- Both writers use language that is partly playful (e.g. Fisher beginning 'Spring is a fertile time', and the humorously exaggerated tone-setting 'orgy of style', and Shaw's suggestion that the bird was 'nailed ... to the lady's temple').
- Fisher covers a range of incidents and celebrity moments (e.g. Björk's egg-laying); Shaw focuses on one incident at the opera, and backs it up with a memory of the theatre.
- Fisher uses visual detail for entertainment value; Shaw uses it more critically, and sharply, in an emotive way, to emphasise the offensiveness of dead birds as fashion accessories.

PAPER 2 SECTION B: WRITING [p. 87]

Mid-level response:

At school we have to wear uniform and dress in a conventional way, day in, day out – the same old navy blue jumpers and grey skirts or trousers. It's dull but practical, and avoids making difficult decisions every morning. However, you might think that on 'mufti days' students would jump at the chance to be individual and show off their style. Instead of that, what they mostly wear is just a different kind of uniform: jeans, designer t-shirts, etc. The fact is, no one wants to stand out and look like a freak. Perhaps there is the occasional Goth, but they are just wearing a different uniform, playing safe, not expressing themselves.

Fashion is actually ridiculous a great deal of the time. Yet people more or less stick to it because they want to be part of a particular set. Teenage girls wear heels so high it looks like they'll fall off them, boys wear their jeans so low that they're always about to fall down. Hoodies are supposed to be cool, but really they are just a disguise – either a real one so that the wearer can commit a crime without being identified, or a mental one because they want to hide who they are, not display it.

The worst thing about clothes is the way people get mocked for what they wear. Girls get called all sorts for having their skirts too short, boys get teased for wearing the wrong make of jeans. It is all just another way for humans to show themselves off as better than others, like peacocks spreading out their feathers in a display.

I think it was King Charles who first wore high heels – because he was short, but now we have tall women tottering about on them because of him. It is simply stupid. Even jeans, the commonest clothing in the western world, started off as hard-wearing practical work clothes, not fashion wear. People wore them to identify with the poor.

In my view, clothes should be practical: hard-wearing and comfortable. I don't want to wear a mini-skirt and skimpy top on a December night, just because it looks good. On the other hand, if I'm going up a mountain I want a proper waterproof, not a leather jacket. Fashion is for those who are frightened of being left out of the in-crowd. It certainly has nothing to do with individual expression.

Comment

This response makes a clear, coherent case, with some use of figurative language and some language devices (e.g. parallelism in 'so high ... so low') and lists of three. The structure is effective, moving from the personal example of school uniform, to a logical conclusion.

A 'good' level response needs:

- Some more interesting language choices
- More use of effective techniques, such as imagery and emotive language
- A more vivid use of details – such as what people wear

High-level response

Fashionable self-expression is not just for showing off – it's the first instinct of human life. From the earliest caveman who had the idea of leaving the paws on his leopard skin, to the first cavalier who had his tailor cut slits in his velvet doublet to reveal his silk shirt underneath, humans have always wanted to show their individual style. Of course, it's partly about showing off in other ways. The caveman wanted to say, 'I'm rough and tough enough to hunt leopards'. The cavalier wanted to impress his foot soldiers, and his fellow officers, to show that he could buy all that fancy outfitting. And just as in those times, the dedicated follower of fashion nowadays wants to impress as well as express.

But it's not that simple. Clothes are about two opposing human needs: individuality, on the one hand, and the urge to merge, on the other. If I wear jeans and a t-shirt, I'm merging into the crowd, becoming one with the great mass of humanity – which we all want. However, if I slash my jeans, wear a rhinestone-studded belt, and paint 'Eat the rich' across my t-shirt, I'm suddenly an individual. Like Wally of the 'Where's Wally?' books, I'm one of the crowd, but if you look closely, you can see how I stand out from it.

So, it may be fashionable – ironically – to mock the excesses of fashion, and even more of celebs like Lady Gaga, with her meat dress, but these all express a normal human need. Moreover, it is actually quite a useful need. Just as medieval soldiers knew who to hack to pieces by what coat of arms they had on their tunic, we modern, civilised types know who we might have things in common with by what they are wearing. Cut-off leather jerkin with half-inch studs and oily jeans? Mmm ... perhaps not quite my sort. Tweed jacket and leather elbows – well, not quite me either.

So, clothes are so much more than just for covering up and keeping warm: they identify us, gain us membership to the right club, and give us a chance to shout out our individuality all at once. What a brilliant invention. Chimpanzees don't know what they're missing!

Comment

A well argued, well structured response that uses anecdote, entertaining examples and some effective

visual details, as well as language devices such as rhetorical question, and connectives that help the flow of the text.

A 'very high' level response needs:

- Some slightly more interesting word choices (e.g. 'exhibit' for 'show')
- More effective language devices (e.g. find a better way to begin the final paragraph and avoid repeating 'So')
- Some further use of descriptive adjectives (e.g. 'bright idea', 'showy silk shirt', 'dangerous leopards').

CHAPTER 7

HOW TO COMMENT ON TEXTS AND USE QUOTATIONS [p. 88]

1 For example: *Meena describes how the Tollington women 'snarl and send death rays to each other', showing their mutual dislike.*

2 For example:

- *The author reveals that the main character …*
- *In this scene Shakespeare demonstrates …*
- *As events unfold, the audience perceives …*
- *The sense of fear is conveyed by …*

3 Answers will vary.

WRITING ABOUT SETTINGS AND CONTEXTS [p. 90]

1–4 Answers will vary.

HOW TO WRITE ABOUT CHARACTERS [p. 92]

1–4 Answers will vary.

HOW TO WRITE ABOUT THEMES [p. 94]

1–5 Answers will vary.

WRITING ABOUT STRUCTURE AND PLOT [p. 96]

1–3 Answers will vary.

COMMENTING ON KEY LITERARY TECHNIQUES [p. 98]

1 Joe is very strong and perhaps even heroic.

2 The adverb and verb create a shocking image using sound as well as sight.

3 For example: *The use of 'Sir' and 'my master' implies that the speaker is a servant and respects the person he is addressing, yet his rhetorical questions suggest that he is challenging the listener's opinion. The simple simile 'like a rat' is appropriate for a servant and conveys his revulsion for the man he is describing. His passing 'a hand over his face' suggests that that he finds this situation stressful.*

CHAPTER 8

WRITING ABOUT AN EXTRACT AND THEN THE WHOLE TEXT [p. 102]

1–3 Answers will vary.

TRACING THEMES, VIEWPOINTS AND PERSPECTIVES [p. 104]

1–3 Answers will vary.

TACKLING SHAKESPEARE'S LANGUAGE [p. 106]

1 Answers will vary.

2 Imagery:

- Shakespeare uses a metaphor in which Juliet is seen as a bright, dangling earring (such as a pearl). Night is personified as having a cheek and a simile compares Juliet's brightness against the 'cheek of night' with that of an earring against the dark skin of an Ethiopian.
- These images show that Romeo has fallen in 'love at first sight' with Juliet. The multiple images suggest that he is overwhelmed.
- He is imaginative and fanciful, rather than practical and down to earth.

3 Answers will vary.

CHAPTER 9

TYPES OF QUESTION AND HOW TO RESPOND TO THEM [p. 110]

1 *How* does *Golding* use *Piggy* to *explore* ideas about *civilisation* in Lord of the Flies?

Write about:

- how Golding *presents* the character of *Piggy*
- how Golding uses *Piggy* to *explore* ideas about *civilisation*.

2 Answers will vary.

TRACING THEMES AND CHARACTERS ACROSS A TEXT [p. 112]

1–2 Answers will vary.

TACKLING MODERN DRAMA STRUCTURES [p. 114]

1–3 Answers will vary.

CHAPTER 10

KEY POETIC TECHNIQUES [p. 118]

1 Stressed syllables:

She <u>put</u> my <u>arm</u> about her <u>waist</u>,
*   And <u>made</u> her <u>smooth</u> white <u>shoulder</u> <u>bare</u>,*
And <u>all</u> her <u>yellow</u> <u>hair</u> displaced,
*   And, <u>stooping</u>, <u>made</u> my <u>cheek</u> lie <u>there</u>.*

The smooth, natural rhythm lulls readers into a false sense of security, which is the opposite of 'The Charge of the Light Brigade'.

2 The similes are all from the natural world, in which he spends his working life. The bride herself is young, unsophisticated and 'wild'.

3 For example: *The 'tedious riddles' simile suggests that the woman still cannot understand the speaker, or what went wrong in their relationship, but that she can no longer be bothered to make the effort.*

4 For example: *The rhythm limps along falteringly, rather than going smoothly, suggesting the awkwardness of the meeting, and the speaker's tired sadness in describing it. Half-rhymes suggest a half-connection between the couple, or a failed one. In the last line the rhythm accentuates the alliterative linking of 'lost' and 'love'.*

COMPARING POEMS [p. 120]

1 For example ('Love and relationships' cluster):

'Eden Rock'	'Mother Any Distance'
Summary: Poet pictures his parents and dog waiting for him on far side of a stream beyond 'Eden Rock'. Mother get ready for picnic. They encourage him to cross.	Poet describes mother helping him measure his new home, holding 'zero-end' of tape measure. He climbs to the loft and contemplates the 'endless sky'.
Symbolism: Stream divides life and death. Eden is paradise. They are dead, but relaxed, and reassure him that death is easy. Mother offers nourishment.	New home is freedom of independence – liberating but frightening: he could 'fall or fly'. He cannot bring himself to cut off from mother. She is 'Anchor'; he is 'kite'. Or she will not let go ('still pinch ...').
Mood: Dreamy, relaxed. Not explicit that parents are dead. Also homely, affectionate – small details of clothes and picnic. Present tense.	Sense of poised tension: 'something has to give'. Ambivalence about freedom: 'acres' and 'prairies' ironic. Also present tense.

Techniques: No similes or metaphors, but affectionate use of precise visual details – clothes (dress, hat), picnic (HP Sauce with paper cork).	Central metaphor of 'spool of tape' connecting mother-son like umbilical cord (note 'feeding'). Other metaphors: freedom vs. insecurity; e.g. 'Anchor', 'Kite' and 'space-walk'.
Metre and form: Four-line stanzas of loose iambic pentameter suggest orderly calm. Rhyme scheme of half-rhymes (e.g. 'bank ... think') suggests half connection to dead parents.	No metre or form, apart from three stanzas: suggests uncertainty of freedom. Only occasional rhymes (e.g. 'pinch ... inch').

For example ('Power and conflict' cluster):

'War Photographer'	'Bayonet Charge'
Summary: Pictures photographer developing photo in dark room in 'rural England'. Developing image reminds him of dying man. Poet imagines magazine readers briefly moved by photos.	Describes terrified soldier charging over field into enemy fire, forgetting patriotism and honour, desperate to reach safety.
Mood: Dark (as in 'dark room') and religious, as if room a Catholic shrine. Ambivalence: he 'has a job to do', but is it pointless? Hands 'tremble' but later he 'stares impassively'. Has he lost ability to feel? Traumatised?	Mood is urgent – of the moment. Immediate physical experience: discomfort – 'raw-seamed hot khaki'; danger – 'dazzled with rifle fire'. One aim: get out of line of fire.
Techniques: Ambiguity of imagery reflects uncertainty of poem; e.g. 'Solutions slop': chemical developing solutions, and political. Are political solutions pointless? Simile compares dark room to church and him to priest.	Imagery all underlines soldier's experience; e.g. metaphor 'Bullets smacking the belly out of the air' – could also smack the air out of his belly; simile 'numb as a smashed arm' signals that his arm could be smashed.
Form: Poem orderly, like the photos, as if trying to contain emotional damage. List of 'Belfast. Beirut. Phnom Penh.' Places of conflict, as if all same, blurring into each other.	Free verse reflects desperate, disorderly charge of soldier. List of 'King, honour, human dignity, etcetera', as if none matter any more.

2 'Bayonet Charge': *'The patriotic tear that had brimmed in his eye / Sweating like molten iron from the centre of his chest'.* Refers to feelings on signing up. Transformed to overwhelming fear, as if he can already feel a bullet in his chest.

'In what cold clockwork of the stars and the nations / Was he the hand pointing that second?' Pictures fate as uncaring and mechanical; he is compelled to play a part. He cannot resist moving forward, like clock hand, or time.

'Poppies': Metaphor describing poppy on the blazer suggests injured soldier jerking uncontrollably and blood spurting. A blockade is a military defence. Could also refer to her blocking her feelings. Metaphor for his spiky hair is realistic, but also indicates emotional self-protection. Neither mother nor son can afford to give in to feelings.

'Walking Away': *'like a satellite / Wrenched from its orbit':* boy has been like a satellite orbiting closely round father; now he is pulled away to school. 'Wrenched' could refer to father's feelings.

'eddying away / Like a winged seed loosened from its parent stem': 'eddying' suggests circular river current; boy's emotional departure not direct, but inevitable. Seed simile suggests both loss and new hope.

'Follower': *'globed like a full sail strung'* describes shape of father's shoulders bending over plough, and perhaps shirt filling with wind. Ship simile portrays father as explorer, powerful.

'Mapping the furrow exactly' continues explorer metaphor. Boy sees father as skilled and knowing his way through life.

3 Power and conflict option:

Hughes conveys the intense urgency and terror of battle. The 'patriotic tear' that the soldier had on signing up for the army has become an intense sense of terror, 'sweating', as he is sweating in fear, and like iron in his chest, as if he has already been shot or bayoneted. Hughes also pictures the soldier as a victim of uncaring, mechanical fate, and international politics, compelled to move forward like the hand of a clock. 'Second' conveys urgency – he could die any moment.

Weir's imagery is more restrained, reflecting the need of mother and son to be restrained as he leaves. She cannot help but use imagery implying her fears for his being injured or dying in battle, but she has to block her feelings. The needlework on his blazer is a feminine symbol for this. (Weir is a textile designer.) He is like other young men, hair fashionably gelled, but the metaphor of thorns indicates that she can no longer mother him as she once did: he would now resist her.

Love and relationships option:

In 'Walking Away', Lewis uses imagery that suggests a painful yet inevitable separation between father and son. The simile 'like a satellite / Wrenched from its orbit' suggests that the boy has been like a satellite orbiting round his father, never far from him; now he is being pulled away to school. 'Wrenched' could refer to the father's feelings more than the boy's. In the combined metaphor and simile of 'eddying away / Like a winged seed loosened from its parent stem', 'eddying' suggests circular currents in the river: the boy's emotional departure is gradual and indirect, but the river's flow will inevitably carry him away. However, the seed simile suggests both loss and the hope of new growth.

The imagery of 'Follower' focuses more on the poet's memory of how, as a boy, he admired his father. 'His shoulders globed like a full sail strung' describes the shape of his father's shoulders bending over the plough, and perhaps his shirt filling with wind. The ship simile suggests that the boy sees his father as a powerful explorer. 'Mapping the furrow exactly' continues this metaphor. The boy sees his father as a skilled man who knows his way through life and the world.

CHAPTER 11

TACKLING AN UNSEEN POEM [p. 124]

1 For example: *Hardy uses the symbolism of a bird building a nest in a 'leafless tree' to represent a poor man who cannot afford a comfortable home for his new wife and is mocked ('twitted') by others for it. He compares the speaker with those who inherit money and advantages, symbolised by 'an evergreen nesting-tree'. They are not mocked like him.*

2 Answers will vary. However, students might comment on Hardy's use of framing – using a speaker who himself is unhappy and 'snow-bound', 'wearily waiting', overhearing a bird speaking. The narrative creates an effective setting. However, a modern reader may find the use of a talking bird unconvincing.

3 For example: *The bird is mocked ('twitted') for marrying without the means to support a wife, the strong adjective 'reckless' suggesting that he is at fault and even deserves to lose his wife. The short exclamation 'But alas!' conveys a strong sense of regret, and the verbs in the phrase 'waned and died' are simple but effective in creating a sense of loss and disappointment. The conversational 'Ah' introducing the final stanza expresses strong regret, and there is a sense of bitterness when the speaker compares his own situation with those born with advantages, symbolised by 'an evergreen nesting-tree'.*

COMPARING UNSEEN POEMS

1 For example: *In the Hardy poem, the limitations are financial. The bird speaks in the voice of an ordinary working man, using simple and even colloquial language such as 'twitted', meaning 'mocked'. In the Brontë poem, there is a strong sense of the speaker sympathising with a real bird limited by being held in a cage. She very effectively compares the freedom that the bird might have had, in the pleasantly suggestive 'sunny mead and shady grove', and the expansive mood of 'rolling sea', with the language used to describe its actual situation: 'prison ... wires ... despair'. Hardy's poem makes a point about social inequality; Brontë expresses the sadness of the lonely through her deep feelings for the unfortunate dove.*

CHAPTER 12

PAPER 1, SECTION A: EXTRACT QUESTIONS ON SHAKESPEARE [p. 131]

MACBETH

- Only Macbeth can see Banquo's ghost: he is either psychic or suffering from guilt-stricken delusions.
- He challenges the ghost, rather than fleeing from it – suggesting bravery.
- He insists that he is as brave as any man, and could face a rhino or fierce tiger: he just cannot face the ghost – or his own ghost. He is very concerned about his masculinity.
- He has proven himself a brave warrior and, at one time, a loyal follower of Duncan.
- He is ambitious and also susceptible to Lady Macbeth's taunts about his masculinity. Therefore he allows himself to be led by her and by the Witches.
- He earns the title 'tragic hero' in the end by taking responsibility for his deeds.

ROMEO AND JULIET

- Juliet has bravely followed the Friar's plan to avoid having to marry Paris, and to be with her husband, Romeo, by taking a sleeping draught.
- Much of the speech is made up of questions – showing uncertainty and insecurity.
- Her speech is fragmented. She interrupts herself with 'O, if I wake', suggesting her great agitation – hardly surprising in the vault, and about to take a mystery potion.
- Shakespeare shows her as a brave girl, prepared to go against the wishes of her parents, and against the longstanding Capulet-Montague feud, for the love of Romeo.
- She is loving and passionate, and hates the fact that Romeo has to leave her, as shown by her insistence that the 'lark' they hear at dawn is a 'nightingale' (bird of night).

- Her suicide is tragic – undertaken because Romeo is dead and she will not remarry.

THE TEMPEST

- Prospero seems full of hatred towards Caliban, calling him 'lying slave' and 'Filth', and saying only whipping will do him any good.
- His control of Caliban could be seen as justified – Caliban tried to rape Miranda, but a modern audience might also compare Prospero with a colonial power.
- Prospero is harsh towards Caliban, but also quite harsh to Ariel, whom he has enslaved.
- Prospero causes the shipwreck, but ensures that no one is hurt.
- He severely tests Ferdinand. This could be for Miranda's good, or because he is a jealous parent who does not want to lose her.
- In the end he forgives those who have wronged him, and renounces magical power to return to his worldly responsibilities.

THE MERCHANT OF VENICE

- Salarino cannot believe that Shylock will insist on his agreement with Antonio and take his 'pound of flesh'.
- Speech shows that Shylock, despite being a merchant, is strongly motivated by revenge. He wants Antonio's flesh even if it is only good for fish bait.
- Shylock's list of grievances against Antonio argues that he is justified; it goes on to become a persuasive attack on anti-Semitism and racial prejudice.
- Shylock loses our sympathy when he insists on his 'pound of flesh', and on taking it in such a way as to kill Antonio.
- Portia, posing as a judge, puts forward a strong case for mercy in her 'quality of mercy' speech; Shakespeare opposes this ideal to revenge.
- It could be argued that in the end Portia, Antonio and the Duke take revenge on Shylock.

MUCH ADO ABOUT NOTHING

- Beatrice and Benedick enter into competitive, mutually insulting banter as soon as they see each other again after Benedick's return. Beatrice says no one listens to Benedick. He calls her 'Lady Disdain' and pretends to be only mildly interested when he finds she is still alive.
- Benedick claims that all ladies love him, but he loves 'none'; Beatrice matches this by saying 'I am of your humour for that': she is equally opposed to marrying.
- Their humour is well-matched, and shows similar temperaments: neither seems to be conventionally romantic – despite which they are tricked into

falling in love. This reflects Shakespearean comedy being largely about marriage as a social harmoniser.
- They both lose a certain amount of dignity when they fall in love, being mocked by other characters, but they never complain.
- Benedick shows himself more seriously suited when he agrees to challenge Claudio because of his humiliation of Hero, Beatrice's cousin, which, in Elizabethan terms, reflects on Beatrice.
- Both are loyal friends who want to see justice: they deserve each other.

JULIUS CAESAR

- Cassius resents Caesar's growing power, and speaks ironically of him as a Colossus, and he and Brutus as 'petty men' who 'peep about' like frightened children.
- Shakespeare addresses a popular debate of the time: are we ruled by fate, represented here by astrology ('our stars'), or by ourselves?
- Cassius insists that they only have themselves to blame if they remain 'underlings'.
- Storms and odd behaviour in the animal kingdom (mentioned in Plutarch, Shakespeare's historical source) seem to be omens pointing to disturbing political events.
- The soothsayer warns Caesar ('Beware the Ides of March'), and Calpurnia wants him to stay at home. Caesar seems to accept fate when he asks, 'What can be avoided / Whose end is purposed by the mighty gods?'
- Shakespeare seems to leave the question open.

PAPER 1, SECTION B: EXTRACT QUESTIONS ON THE NINETEENTH-CENTURY NOVEL [p. 133]

ROBERT LOUIS STEVENSON: THE STRANGE CASE OF DR JEKYLL AND MR HYDE

- Jekyll is presented as troubled ('grew pale to the very lips'); he is 'painfully situated'.
- That he can only refuse Utterson's help, and cannot benefit by confiding in him argues that his case is very serious and deserves sympathy.
- Jekyll's gratitude to Utterson, just for wanting to help, shows how much he needs sympathy, and makes him more deserving.
- Jekyll is respectable and has many friends. The fact that Utterson is Jekyll's friend and wants to help him is itself a recommendation.
- Jekyll is a risk-taker and sees Lanyon as 'hidebound' – making him both appealing, especially to modern readers, yet guilty of hubris (ambitious pride).
- Jekyll is a truth-seeker, and believes in the dual nature of man ('not truly one, but truly two'). Could argue that his real crime is honesty about

his own darker side. We sympathise because in the end he suffers and is condemned to lose his better self to Hyde – almost as if damned.

CHARLES DICKENS: *A CHRISTMAS CAROL*

- Scrooge is terrified by the ghost. We see his desire to change, and be saved from the fate of dying with no one caring, with his appeal, 'Say it is thus ...' that 'the ends will change'.
- Words 'crept' and 'trembling' show that Scrooge has become afraid, a prelude to change, rather than 'Hard and sharp as flint'.
- Insists 'I am not the man I was' and reasons that there must be hope for the ghost to show him the vision of his grave.
- Over the course of the novella he changes from being mean, scorning the spirit of Christmas (e.g. in his rudeness to Fred in Chapter 1), to being joyful and generous.
- The Ghost of Christmas Past shows how Scrooge has become what he is. Christmas Present shows him poor families, especially Cratchits, and Want and Ignorance (reflecting Dickens's social views). But Scrooge only completes his change when made aware of his own mortality.
- Finally Dickens shows a humorous but sympathetic view of Scrooge, so happy he is 'giddy as a drunken man', ending the story with a strong moral conclusion.

CHARLES DICKENS: *GREAT EXPECTATIONS*

- Pip and friends are close to getting Magwitch onto the steamer so he can escape to the country and avoid arrest. Dickens creates suspense by leaving it until they have almost managed to do this for an officer to challenge them.
- Action happens swiftly, 'before we knew what they were doing'. Sentence beginning 'This caused ...' emphasises rapid events, like the steamer paddles turning, accentuated by a list with 'and' repeated: 'and I heard them ... and heard the order ... and heard them stop ...'.
- Phrases such as 'In the same moment', 'quite frantically', 'white with terror', 'felt the boat sink' create suspense and drama.
- Novel begins with drama – when Pip meets convict in the graveyard. Develops with Pip being made to steal a file and food, and then with the convicts being hunted.
- Mrs Havisham presents a different kind of Gothic drama.
- Often there is the threat of violence, either veiled, as with Jaggers, or openly physical, e.g. vengeful Orlick lures Pip to the sluice-house.

CHARLOTTE BRONTË: *JANE EYRE*

- Jane makes a mistake in honestly saying 'Psalms are not interesting'. Her honesty in not humouring Brocklehurst contradicts Mrs Reed's claims.
- Brocklehurst's reply shows his ignorant lack of sympathy with children and his extreme religious views (not unusual at the time), as does his reference to fire and brimstone.
- Mrs Reed's accusation of 'deceit' and Brocklehurst's unquestioning belief in it are unjust. Jane has to battle prejudice. Mrs Reed is 'already obliterating hope' for her.
- Jane's first problem is in being (apparently) poor – which is why she is sent to Lowood. She is also unloved. As an adult she believes herself too plain for a man to love her.
- Rochester seems to change her fortunes, but her discovery that he is married to Grace Poole dashes Jane's hopes. Her challenge is to behave morally and leave him.
- She manages to avoid marriage to the emotionally cold, repressed St John Rivers. Eventually 'rewarded' by marriage to Rochester.

MARY SHELLEY: *FRANKENSTEIN*

- The Creature appreciates nature. Notices trees 'budding with fresh spring'.
- He saves girl 'with extreme labour', risking own life, and succeeds – only to be shot and wounded by 'rustic'.
- 'Writhed', 'miserable pain', 'shattered' and 'agony' emphasise his suffering. Clearly blames incident for his conversion to 'eternal hatred and vengeance'.
- The Monster is created huge and ugly – likely to cause revulsion; doomed to loneliness unless Frankenstein will make him a partner. Pleads for this and almost gets it – then Frankenstein destroys his work.
- Monster appreciates poetry – e.g. Milton, and seems to identify with Milton's Satan. Intelligent and speaks eloquently.
- Shelley ambiguous. Monster is badly mistreated by Frankenstein and humanity, but he does do some evil things – e.g. framing Justine.

JANE AUSTEN: *PRIDE AND PREJUDICE*

- Elizabeth shows vanity and insensitivity in her negative reaction to Charlotte's engagement. Elizabeth is more attractive than Charlotte, so has more chance of marriage.
- Austen presents Charlotte as marrying for financial support and to avoid spinsterhood, rather than for love – arguably the best a woman in her position could do in Austen's time. Collins simply wants to marry – not concerned about love. It does seem ridiculous for him to propose to two women in three days.

- Novel opens with a line ironically assuming that a single man with a fortune must be looking for a wife – signalling link between marriage and money.
- Austen presents the Bennets as an example of an unhappy marriage. Mr Bennet married an unintelligent woman for her youthful charms.
- Some see purpose of marriage to cement family connections and keep wealth within family – e.g. Lady Catherine. Wickham shows another side of marriage – the opportunist.
- Elizabeth and Darcy make the perfect marriage because they are suited in character and intelligence, despite unequal rank – Austen was making a radical point at the time.

SIR ARTHUR CONAN DOYLE: *THE SIGN OF THE FOUR*

- Sholto is exotic in having an Indian servant, and in living in a 'little sanctum' at odds with the 'sordid and common passage' leading to it.
- First appearance dramatic, framed in 'yellow light', odd looks: 'small man with a very high head, a bristle of red hair all round the fringe of it, and a bald, shining scalp'. Strange simile comparing his head to a 'mountain peak'. Bad teeth.
- Nervous, never still, 'in a perpetual jerk'. Prematurely bald. Strange voice and affected style of speech: 'oasis of art'.
- Exotic, tasteful decor, 'a diamond of the first water'; tiger-skins, rugs, hookah.
- Worries about own health, asking Watson to check his heart. Sensitive about himself but not others – e.g. Miss Morstan's feelings on way to Pondicherry Lodge.
- Elsewhere in novel self-preoccupied. Announces Captain Morstan's death insensitively.

PAPER 2, SECTION A: MODERN PROSE AND DRAMA [p. 135]

J. B. PRIESTLEY: *AN INSPECTOR CALLS*

- Appears at first to be ordinary police inspector, but is more sympathetic to Eva Smith, and makes more moral judgements than a real inspector would.
- Dramatic role is to make each character in turn see their guilt: withholds information and asks questions to make them incriminate themselves.
- This fits with his pursuing 'one line of enquiry at a time', so focus is on one character at a time.
- We learn about Eva Smith from him – background and how she died.
- Mouthpiece for Priestley's moral message of social responsibility: 'fire and blood and anguish' will come 'if men will not learn that lesson'.
- Mystery of who he is, or was – a ghost (ghoul – Goole), voice of conscience. Twist of phone call announcing that an inspector is coming.

WILLY RUSSELL: *BLOOD BROTHERS*

- Identical twins – so should be similar in character and abilities.
- Sensitive scene when they meet as boys. Contrast in speech (Edward 'posh', Mickey working-class Liverpool) and attitudes: Edward offers Mickey sweet. Both equally innocent in discussing 'plate' in Sammy's head.
- Remain friends, despite Mrs Lyons' efforts – threesome with Linda. Edward more confident and sophisticated – encourages Mickey to make Linda his girlfriend.
- Incident with police officer – his attitude towards Mickey and Edward very different.
- Edward going to university is beginning of end for friendship. Edward cannot understand Mickey's situation. Mickey says Edward has never had to grow up.
- Mickey's unemployment, prison, depression, addiction, while Edward becomes a councillor. Russell's message is that 'fate' is really the result of social situation.

ALAN BENNETT: *THE HISTORY BOYS*

- Hector opposes education for exam system. Wants to expand boys' thinking. Special focus on literature and the arts.
- Irwin, a supply teacher, is given job of preparing boys for Oxbridge entrance exams. Encourages boys to be controversial just to impress – to 'pretend' rather than say what they really think. Thinks Hector encourages dull interpretations of history.
- Hector thinks education is for life – opposite of head's view which is that it is just to achieve status (especially for the school).
- Head hires Irwin to bring grammar-school boys up to independent-school level – highlighting social inequalities in education, preserving elitism.
- Hector eccentric. Boys practise subjunctive tense in French by role-play set in a Paris brothel. Also gets them to learn and recite poetry.
- Hector relatively open with the boys – they learn from his personality; Irwin more guarded. Hector treats history, especially the First World War, as a literary context. He believes in power of literature. Irwin glib and cynical: history is 'a performance'. His methods get Posner into Cambridge but fail him in life.

DENNIS KELLY: *DNA*

- Main victim is Adam – tortured and thought killed when he fell through a grille, then found alive, and finally (we assume) actually killed to protect gang.
- Importance of loyalty to gang versus individual morality and compassion; Leah on chimps and bonobos.

- Leaders replaced when they can no longer hold on to position and protect group: John Tate (finds God), Phil (becomes silent), Cathy (even more extreme – cuts off a first year's finger).
- Phil bullies Brian into incriminating postal worker in Adam's death. Bullying connected to refusal to take responsibility. Leah denies group responsible, then says should share blame ('we haven't done anything ... but if we have ...')
- Effects of bullying (e.g. Brian goes mad and eats earth) and question of whether bullied are in any way to blame. Mark and Jan say Adam was 'laughing' and was a 'nutter'.
- Kelly asks, are we chimps or bonobos? Is bullying inevitable in groups – in our DNA?

SIMON STEPHENS: *THE CURIOUS INCIDENT OF THE DOG IN THE NIGHT-TIME*

- Christopher autistic (not made explicit). Brilliant at maths and science but has difficulty 'reading' and relating to people. Cannot empathise and understand what they need to know – e.g. when policeman asks what he is doing in garden.
- Cannot bear to be touched – father (fingertips only), mother, policeman.
- His determination can irritate others – his refusal to drop investigation into who killed Wellington. Sticks to goals.
- Tries not to get involved with other people, like elderly neighbour Mrs Alexander. Interacts to some extent, despite instructions and own reservations.
- Use of Siobahn reading from Christopher's account to narrate. Gives us insight, e.g. 'I find people confusing.'
- Christopher's honesty (but lies to father about investigation); shocked and angered by dishonesty of others – especially Ed saying Judy dead. Heroic effort when he goes to find her – must really care for her.

SHELAGH DELANEY: *A TASTE OF HONEY*

- Main love relationship is mother (Helen) and daughter (Jo). Like a marriage in that they are more equal than in a typical parent–child relationship. Helen neglects Jo, but loves her in her way. Jo criticises Helen but loves her. They bicker like a couple.
- Helen a poor example. Married once before. Conceived Jo in an affair (she 'had nothing better to do'). Peter is a selfish, unfaithful man. Helen seems to want his money, and security. Helen wishes Jo could 'learn from my mistakes'.
- With no father and a neglectful mother, not surprising that Jo is won over by Boy's affection and promises. Boy seems to care for Jo, but does either of them believe he will return to her?

- Ironically, homosexual Geof supports Jo more than anyone else. Even offers to marry her. Says he doesn't mind that she is having another man's baby. Committed to her: 'I'd sooner be dead than away from you.'
- Sad that Helen drives Geof away when he is devoted to Jo, but at least Helen makes an effort for Jo at the end.
- Perhaps Delaney is saying that all relationships are flawed and disappointing, and that all we can expect is temporary sweetness – a 'taste of honey'.

WILLIAM GOLDING: *LORD OF THE FLIES*

- Ralph associated with symbol of conch – standing for democracy, Jack with spear.
- Ralph supports rule of law, protection of younger, weaker boys, and importance of keeping fire alight to be seen and rescued. Jack more interested in hunting.
- Ralph has charisma to become leader, but his rationalism cannot manage boys' deep fears and savage impulses. Reluctant to believe in the beast; Jack exploits fear of beast; says he and 'his' hunters will kill it.
- Ralph wants to preserve adult civilisation, and comes to respect Piggy's intelligence. Jack sees island as opportunity to shed civilised restraints and become a tribal leader ('my tribe'), breaking from Ralph and his few remaining supporters.
- Ralph is kind-hearted; Jack has a powerful streak of cruelty and ruthlessness, rules by fear and intimidation (has Wilfred beaten, perhaps an idea from school). He offers meat; Ralph offers rules. Jack prepared to hunt Ralph to the death.
- When officers arrive, Ralph accepts responsibility – says he is leader; Jack shrinks away. They represent two types of political leader in adult world: democrat and dictator.

AQA ANTHOLOGY: *TELLING TALES*

- In 'Odour of Chrysanthemums', mother speaks firmly to 'sulky', 'resentful, taciturn' boy, then more 'gently'. Sees her husband's self-centredness in him.
- Daughter more sympathetic. Tries to manage mother when she is bitter about husband's drinking. Daughter dreamy about fire and has 'a little rapture' over flower in mother's apron; mother practical, dismissive – perhaps was like daughter once.
- Mother loves children – partly angry with father on their behalf. Tries to protect them (pointlessly) from knowing he is dead ('nothing to make a fuss about').
- In 'The Darkness Out There', teenagers slightly patronising about the old people, but want to help them.

- Mrs Rutter assertive, not slow to give Sandra and Kerry tasks. They are shocked by her account of letting the German airman die, as if in revenge for her husband.
- Children in both stories represent hope: all that is left of the failed marriage in 'Odour of Chrysanthemums', and a more forgiving compassionate view in 'The Darkness Out There'.

GEORGE ORWELL: *ANIMAL FARM*

- Novel is allegory of Russian Revolution and its aftermath. Jones represents tsar and old regime. Napoleon can be seen as Stalin, and Snowball as Trotsky.
- Jones exploited animals; after takeover, Napoleon exploits them instead.
- Pigs (intelligent animals) can be seen as Communist Party elite. Use propaganda and speeches to manipulate animals, and gradually take benefits for themselves – milk and apples, claiming it is for social good.
- Pigs' power and privilege depends on the unquestioning hard work of animals like Boxer, representing Russian peasantry, and obedient savagery of dogs – representing roles of security forces in repressive USSR.
- In the end, pigs become indistinguishable from the men with whom they now do business. They are the new ruling class.
- Orwell's style is simple (he called it a 'fable'), with restrained irony, allowing readers to draw their own conclusions – more effective than being heavy-handed or showing pigs' manipulation and animals' suffering in vivid detail.

KAZUO ISHIGURO: *NEVER LET ME GO*

- Dystopian novel. Clone children brought up at Hailsham to believe they have a special role, and must look after themselves, but not told what. They accept this. Actually society is prejudiced against them – even disgusted.
- Told they must produce art. Accept that this is somehow important. Learn later that this is meant to help argue the case that they are individuals.
- Roy challenges the token system for art going into the gallery: actually a pathetic rebellion in the context of the much larger injustice of cloning for body parts.
- Kathy prides herself on being a good 'carer', minimising the suffering of her 'donors'. She is dutiful in her work, is grateful for small perks, and accepts her fate.
- Ishiguro uses Kathy as first-person narrator: calm voice, sometimes wistful, never rebellious.

- To many readers it would seem strange that even the clones never rebel against being exploited. They accept the euphemism of 'completion' for their early deaths. Ishiguro never describes the network behind the exploitation – making a point about society?

MEERA SYAL: *ANITA AND ME*

- Meena is a first-person narrator, so we find out about her directly through her comments on herself and others. Narrative filters the child's voice through often ironic adult perspective.
- At start, Meena is a liar (or fantasist), who lies to get out of trouble, and to make life more interesting. Also loves drama, e.g. story of hot dog, and her wanting to hear the 'rickshaw story' repeatedly.
- She is naive – believes that Anita's father was a sailor, and easily impressed by charismatic Anita, whose rebelliousness challenges Meena's desire to please her parents.
- Reaches a moral low-point when she steals collection tin from Mr Ormerod and blames Baby.
- Gradually becomes aware of growing racism in village, represented by Sam, and approved of by Anita. Meena very opposed – start of rift with Anita.
- Through knowing Nanima, breaking leg, loss of Anita's friendship, and moment when she chooses to tell the truth to the police, Meena learns to become more secure in her identity, and rejects the idea that she has to choose between two cultures.

STEPHEN KELMAN: *PIGEON ENGLISH*

- He misses father and baby sister Agnes in Ghana – can only keep in touch by Skype; often recalls life in Ghana – presented as innocent and relaxed, though poor.
- Family in debt to thuggish Julius, with his baseball bat, 'the Persuader'. Auntie Sonia has to burn off her fingerprints.
- Is called 'Ghana' by the Dell Farm Crew, but does not seem to experience racism in multicultural society; no mention of any character's ethnicity.
- In some ways has an African attitude to luck and superstition – e.g. his alligator's tooth.
- Pakistani butcher, Nish, and wife deported; mixed response – women mostly concerned about where they will get their meat now. Harrison worries about own family's visa.
- Adapts well to life in UK: mostly happy, but caught up in youth violence.

PAPER 2, SECTION B: COMPARING ANTHOLOGY POEMS [p. 138]

'Mother Any Distance' and 'Before You Were Mine'

- Focus in 'Mother Any Distance' is on poet's feelings about his mother. All we learn about her, perhaps, is that she is reluctant to let go of him, just as he is of her. She still pinches the end of the tape, even outstretched. In 'Before You Were Mine' we learn much more about Duffy's mother. Could even call it a tribute to her. Duffy names her mother's friends, pictures them on the corner, the mother in 'a polka dot dress'.
- Both poems address the mother, but in mood there is more sense of anxiety and the drama of suspense in Armitage. Duffy is affectionately admiring. Her poem is more comfortable.
- Armitage pictures his mother helping him measure his new home. Duffy imagines her mother's life before she became a mother – her dancing, her dreams – 'fizzy, movie tomorrows', her 'high-heeled red shoes'. The picture is glamorous (especially the reference to Monroe) and fictional, perhaps based on a photo.
- Armitage imagery focuses on the tension between his wanting freedom and opportunity and his fear of it; 'acres' and 'prairies' are ironic, as if he has too much space. The tape measure is an umbilical symbol. Most vivid contrast is 'Anchor. Kite': security versus freedom. The tension reaches a peak at the end in the pun of 'hatch' (opening on to roof, and 'hatch' as in baby bird that will 'fall or fly'.
- Duffy uses hardly any figurative language – only 'clear as scent', but the poem is full of images in the broader sense – very visual, painting a picture of the mother in her youth.

'Bayonet Charge' and 'Exposure'

- 'Bayonet Charge' is a snapshot – a moment of extreme violence, fear and tension. A third person, past tense narrative describing the immediate experience of the soldier: uncomfortable uniform, sweat, the rifle's weight, his panicky feelings.
- 'Exposure', is first-person plural (we), present tense, not a narrative but describing the on-going, almost unchanging experience of all the men in the trenches. 'Bayonet Charge' focuses on the survival of one man, 'Exposure' on the ordeal of thousands.
- 'Bayonet Charge' implies reasons for the man signing up: the 'patriotic tear' now seems transformed by fear of death; his reasons for signing up – 'King, honour, human dignity, etcetera' are now made to seem meaningless by being listed like this. 'Exposure' gives reasons for the men being there – 'not otherwise can kind fired burn', but the overall experience still seems futile. They suffer the ordeal of weather ('iced east winds', intensified by alliteration) and waiting (numbing repetition of 'But nothing happens').
- In Owen's poem there is context in the men thinking of home – the home fires made precious by the image of 'dark-red jewels'; in Hughes the context is in the man momentarily wondering about the 'cold clockwork of the stars and the nations', puzzling over the apparent callousness of fate and politics.
- In both poems the men seem neglected and abandoned to their fate.

PAPER 2, SECTION C: UNSEEN POETRY [p. 138]

1 'It Rains'

- Strong sense of weather and place, with opening 'It rains' establishing importance of weather; 'diamonds' metaphor makes rain sound precious.
- Rain reminds him of time when he and his lover were too in love to care about the rain – regarding it as 'kisses'.
- Rain ensures that he is alone: 'nothing stirs', 'none to break', as if this is a moment out of time.
- Stanza 2 looks back to the past love, but although it seems past, remembering makes him 'nearly as happy as possible'. We wonder how happy that is.
- Stanza 3 switches abruptly, with 'Sad, too'; repetition of 'never' emphasises loss. Twilight is part of the setting, as if this is the twilight of his life, and he and his former lover have become ghosts, as in the implied image of the parsley flowers 'ghostly white'.
- Final line magical, suggesting that the past can 'hover' (personification), momentarily coming back to life.
- Partial rhyme scheme suggests partial reconnection with past. Interesting that the rhyme scheme would be more obvious if Stanza 3 began with 'Unless' instead of 'Sad'.

2 'It Rains' and 'The Voice'

- Thomas describes a present moment in which he seems to take comfort from being alone in the rain in a place where he was once with his lover, and from nature. He is 'almost ... happy', and describes the natural beauty evocatively.
- Hardy poem is sadder, focusing on the imagined voice of a lost lover. The rhythm and use of alliteration (e.g. 'much missed', 'call to me, call to me') suggest him trying to stagger on through life without her, her memory and even her voice haunting him.
- Thomas has an element of narrative – the happy, kissing lovers. Hardy implies a decline in his

relationship, with the woman changing from 'one who was all to me'. The 'f' alliteration of 'first' and 'fair' connects the words,

- Both poems contain an element of the past revisiting the present in ghostly form. Hardy, barely daring to believe in the imagined voice, challenges her to appear, creating a vivid picture of her in a beautiful 'air-blue gown'.
- In both poems, we are left to wonder where, or why, the lover has gone. In Hardy, especially, it seems she is dead: 'dissolved' and 'Heard no more'.

- Hardy only uses weather and setting in last two stanzas. He wonders if the voice could just be the breeze. In the final stanza the rhythm changes, slowing down, so the lines echo the poet 'faltering forward', halting, uncertain. Image of 'wind oozing thin through the thorn', accentuated by alliteration, with falling autumnal leaves, is desperately bleak. Poem ends with a return to the woman's voice that will not go away.
- In Thomas, there is a greater sense of the poet being reconciled to the past: he accepts what little he now has – the temporary revisiting of the past in memory - whereas Hardy is bereft.

abstract noun a noun that refers to feelings, concepts, states that do not exist physically (e.g. hope, love)

adjective a word used to describe something or somebody (e.g. 'the **red** hat')

adverb a word used to modify a verb, adjective or another adverb, usually formed by adding 'ly' to an adjective

adverbial a word or phrase that is used in the same way as an adverb, to modify a verb or clause

adverbial clause a clause that functions like an adverb

alliteration where the same sound is repeated in a stretch of language, usually at the beginning of words

anecdote a short, usually entertaining story about a personal experience, used to make a point

auxiliary verb verbs used with other verbs such as 'be', 'do', 'have'; also modal verbs, which express possibility or necessity: 'must', 'shall', 'will', 'could', 'should', 'would', 'can', 'may' and 'might'

bildungsroman a novel about the development of the main character from childhood to adulthood

blank verse poetry that is unrhymed; Shakespeare's plays are mostly written in blank verse

broadsheet a newspaper in a large format, usually considered more serious than 'tabloid' newspapers

cadence the recurring rise and fall of the rhythms of speech; it can also refer to a rhythm that comes at the close of a line or a poem

catharsis the feeling of a release of emotional tension, usually at the end of a play

characterisation the creation of characters in a dramatic work and how they are presented through description, speech and action

clause a special phrase whose head is a verb; a clause can be a complete sentence

cliché an image that is overused and so becomes boring

cliffhanger a dramatic ending to an episode, leaving the audience or reader in suspense

climax the high point of a play, act or story

colloquialism everyday speech used by people in ordinary situations

colon (:) a punctuation mark that precedes a list, or when a character speaks in a play script or an expansion in a sentence

comma splice an error of punctuation in which a comma is used to link two independent clauses

complex sentence a sentence usually made up of a main clause and one or more subordinate clauses

compound adjective a single adjective made of more than one word (e.g. 'four-legged')

compound sentence a sentence made up of two independent clauses joined by a coordinating conjunction

conjunction a word that links two words or phrases together; there are two types: coordinating conjunctions and subordinating conjunctions

connective a word such as 'however' or 'moreover', used to link paragraphs or sentences and show the relationship between them

coordinating conjunction a conjunction that links two words or phrases together as an equal pair

dash (–) a punctuation mark used to set off a word or phrase after an independent clause

dénouement the final part of a story, play or film

determiner a word that specifies a noun as known or unknown (e.g. 'the', 'a', 'this', 'my', 'some')

dialect accent and vocabulary, varying by region and social background

dialogue speech and conversation between characters

direct speech words that are actually spoken by a character in a novel or story

discourse marker a word or phrase that helps organise speech into sections (e.g. 'well', 'so', 'anyway')

dramatic irony when the reader or audience is aware of something that a character in a novel or play is not

ellipses (…) a series of dots to show where words have been deliberately left out of a sentence ('ellipsis' is the singular)

emotive language language chosen especially to create an emotional response in the reader

explicit refers to information that is stated openly in a piece of writing

extended metaphor in poetry, a metaphor that continues some aspect of the image; it may continue into the next line or throughout the poem

fable a story, usually with animal characters, that conveys a lesson or moral

figurative language words or phrases that are used to express a meaning that is different from their literal meaning

finite clause a clause that makes sense on its own as a complete sentence

flashback a scene or part of a play, novel or film that goes back in time to reveal past events

flash-forwards a scene or part of a play, novel or film that goes forward in time, beyond the main story

foreshadowing a hint of what is to come in a work of poetry, fiction or drama

framing a story within a story

genre a type of story, based on its style (e.g. horror, science fiction, romance)

homophones words that sound the same but that have different spellings and meanings

iambic pentameter a line of poetry consisting of five iambic feet (iambic means each foot has a weak syllable followed by a strong one)

imagery descriptive language that uses images to make actions, objects and characters more vivid in the reader's mind

implicit refers to information that is hinted at or suggested in a piece of writing, rather than being stated openly

in media res when a story starts in the middle of events

indirect object a noun phrase referring to a person or object that is affected by the action of the verb but is not the main object

irony deliberately saying one thing when you mean another, usually in a humorous, sarcastic or sometimes thoughtful way

lyric poem a poem expressing the emotions and thoughts of the speaker, often exploring a single feeling or idea

main clause a sentence contains at least one main clause, which makes sense on its own

metaphor when one thing is used to describe another to create a striking or unusual image

metre the pattern of stressed and unstressed syllables in a line of verse

minor sentence a sentence that is grammatically incomplete, perhaps not containing a subject or verb

mnemonic a memory aid that can help with remembering spelling, for example

modifier a word or phrase that alters the meaning of another

monologue a long speech by a character in a play, used to move the plot along or explain things that the audience might not otherwise realise

mood the tone or atmosphere created by an artistic work

motif a recurring image in a story or poem

motivation the reason that a character in a novel or play acts the way they do

narrative viewpoint the point of view from which a story is told; this might be first person ('I') or third person ('he', 'she', 'they')

non-finite clause a clause that cannot stand on its own as a complete sentence but which relies on the main clause to make sense

noun phrase a phrase with a noun as its head

novella narrative prose longer than a short story, but shorter than a novel

onomatopoeia a word that suggests its meaning through its sound (for example 'meow', 'squelch')

parallelism achieving contrast by repeating a grammatical formation

participle English verbs have two participles: present (e.g. 'talking') and past (e.g. 'talked')

personification describing an object or idea as though it was human, with human feelings and attributes

phrase a group of words that are grammatically connected

prefix a letter or a group of letters added to the start of a word, which alters its grammatical form and sometimes its meaning ('**aero**plane', '**il**legal')

preposition a word that tell the reader the relationship between things or people, such as 'near', 'by', 'under', 'towards' etc.

prepositional phrase a phrase with a preposition as its head, followed by a noun, pronoun or noun phrase

pronoun words that are used instead of nouns (e.g. personal pronouns: 'it', 'they', 'this', 'she', 'him')

prose the natural flow of speech used in novels and other works, unlike poetry which has a more emphasised rhythmic structure

protagonist the main or a major character

refrain repeated lines or groups of words that convey the same meaning

register the style of language based on choice of vocabulary and grammar

relative pronoun a word used to link a clause to a noun or pronoun (e.g. 'which', 'that', 'who')

reported speech an account of what has been said, without using the exact words spoken

resolution the end of a conflict, when issues are worked out

rhetorical question a question asked for effect, rather than to elicit an answer

rhyming couplet a couplet (two paired lines) that rhymes

round brackets () used to include extra information or an afterthought

semicolon (;) a type of punctuation that links two idea, events or pieces of information

setting where and when the action of a story takes place

sibilance strongly stressed consonants that make a hissing sound when spoken aloud

simile when one thing is compared directly with another using 'like' or 'as'

simple sentence a sentence with one main clause, usually containing a subject, verb and object

soliloquy a dramatic techniques that allows a character to speak as if thinking aloud, revealing their inner thoughts and intentions to the audience

sonnet a fourteen-line verse with a rhyming couplet at the end

square brackets ([ ]) a form of punctuation mainly used to enclose words not said by the original speaker or writer to clarify (e.g. 'He [the red fox] slipped away, unseen.')

stage directions advice printed from time to time in the text of a play, giving instructions or information to the actors, or on setting and special effects

Standard English the form of English most widely accepted as the conventional form

stanza a group or pattern of lines forming a verse

subordinate clause a clause that is secondary to another part of the sentence

subordinating conjunction a conjunction that introduces a subordinate clause

subplot a secondary storyline that supports the main one, often by reinforcing the theme

suffix a letter or a group of letters added to the end of a word, which alters its grammatical form ('sweet**ness**', 'advent**ure**')

symbol something that represents something else, usually with meanings that are widely known (e.g. a dove as a symbol of peace)

tautology saying the same thing twice over in different words, usually as an error of style (e.g. 'They spoke together simultaneously.')

theme an idea running through a work of literature or art

tone see mood

topic sentence a sentence that expresses the main idea of a paragraph, sometimes the first of the paragraph

triad list of three

tricolon using three words or phrases in a row for effect